I Hate It Here, Please Vote for Me

I Hate It Here, Please Vote for Me

Essays on Rural Political Decay

MATTHEW FERRENCE

WEST VIRGINIA UNIVERSITY PRESS · MORGANTOWN

Quote from "Autumn Begins in Martins Ferry, Ohio" from *Above the River: The Complete Poems and Selected Prose*, © 1971 by James Wright. Published by Wesleyan University Press. Used by permission.

ISBN 978-1-959000-27-3 (paperback) / 978-1-959000-28-0 (ebook)

Library of Congress Cataloging-in-Publication Data
Names: Ferrence, Matthew J., author.
Title: I hate it here, please vote for me : essays on rural political decay / Matthew Ferrence.
Other titles: Essays on rural political decay
Description: First edition. | Morgantown : West Virginia University Press, 2024. | Includes
    bibliographical references. | Summary: "In essays on showing goats at the county fair,
    planting native grasses in the front lawn, the political power of poetry, and getting
    wiped out in an election, Ferrence offers a counter-narrative to the stereotypes of
    monolithic rural American voters" --Provided by publisher.
Identifiers: LCCN 2024009294 | ISBN 9781959000273 (paperback) | ISBN
    9781959000280 (ebook)
Subjects: LCSH: Ferrence, Matthew J. | Political candidates--Pennsylvania--Crawford
    County--Biography. | Crawford County (Pa.)--Politics and government--21st century.
    | Crawford County (Pa.)--Biography. | Political candidates--Pennsylvania--Biography.
    | Pennsylvania--Politics and government--21st century. | Appalachians
    (People)--Pennsylvania--Biography.
Classification: LCC F157.C77 F47 2024 | DDC 974.8/97092 [B]--dc23/eng/20240313
LC record available at https://lccn.loc.gov/2024009294

Book and cover design by Than Saffel / WVU Press
Cover image: *Looking westward along Chestnut Street from just past the corner of Cottage Street in downtown Meadville, Pennsylvania on an October 2022 afternoon* by Andre Carrotflower. Licensed under the Creative Commons Attribution-Share Alike 4.0 International license.

Cries and whispers. A bang or a whimper. Whatever the case, if we want to be heard, we must raise our voice, or lower it.

—Mary Ruefle, *Madness, Rack, and Honey*

CONTENTS

ACKNOWLEDGMENTS

A book is written in community. My deepest thanks and appreciation to those who make up the neighborhood of these essays:

Each and every person at or once at WVU Press, who together make up the absolute model of what a small press oughta be. Derek Krissoff, who made the reclamation of this project possible after an early demise. I'll tell you about it if we ever have a beer together. Sarah Munroe and Sara Georgi, generous participants in my literary community and expert shepherds for this book in different stages. Particular thanks to Than Saffel and Natalie Homer, who keep going when the going is as the going has gotten.

The editors and staff of *Copper Nickel*, *Northern Appalachian Review*, *Cutbank*, *The Daily Yonder*, and *Blue Mesa Review*, all of whom published essays that served as prototype beta-versions of portions of this book.

Christina Kljunich, who became an expert on William McKinley, Alice Bentley, and the chaos of my early drafting process.

The friends who stepped up and helped me when I took on the folly of political candidacy, with particularly notable efforts from Ian Binnington, Kristy Gnibus, Brad Hersh, Amanda Rhoda Mangine, John Mangine, Melissa Mencotti, David Miller,

Peggy Mogush, Jenny Kawata, Angela Keysor, Shanna Kirschner, Adrienne Krone, Brian Miller, Tamara Misner, Eric Straffin, and Lisa Whitenack.

Always and most of all, Jennifer, Jozef, Sebastien. All of the things.

I Hate It Here, Please Vote for Me

★ **ONE** ★

WELCOME TO THE PARTY

November, just a week since the 2018 midterms. The weather had taken a quick turn on election night, high winds that blew late-changing leaves off the trees and revealed bare bony fingers. Drifts of leaves packed the gutters, and winter arrived all at once. This shouldn't have been a surprise, here in northwestern Pennsylvania, snow country, where the lake effect dumps a foot at a time and keeps it coming for months.

Early November marks the annual turn toward snow around here, an all-at-once descent into months of gray cold. Election Day always seems like an inevitable meteorological turning point, always toward grim relentless winter. Am I spinning a metaphor here, an alignment between winter's dimmed light and the relentless deluge of right-wing politics that buries the hope of rural progress? Probably. It also is cold in this memory.

In front of me, paint flaked from the front door of the Crawford County Democratic Committee headquarters. More paint peeled from the window trim, and sheet plastic had been stapled to the inside of the frame to block drafts. The plastic created a milky backdrop for a few candidate signs, still hanging as evidence of elections just passed. None of them won, or even came close. A donkey-emblazoned vinyl banner drooped over the front door, and the porch reeked of stale cigarette smoke.

Inside HQ, a sun-faded cardboard Barack Obama greeted visitors to the meeting room. Metal chairs were packed closely on a dingy linoleum floor. A bulletin board carried various bits of Democratic Party flotsam, candidate signs, and lots of blue, a political team-pride vibe. Election-night posterboard clung to the wall, black magic marker tallying the losses. Local Democrats were eviscerated in bids to unseat Republican incumbents in the state senate and US House. The splits were sixty to forty for Congress and seventy to thirty for state senate in Crawford County, and in the county's three state house races, Republican incumbents won without even facing a Democratic opponent. That happens more often than not, races left unopposed because, really, what's the point?

All of it, the losses, the empty ballot lines, and the relentless domination of rural politics by an increasingly unhinged version of the GOP, led me to Democratic HQ that day. Like so many people, I'd grown tired and angry of politicians who signed onto the reality-bending ugliness of demagoguery. On the national landscape, Trump was deep in the throes of becoming exactly what reasonable people feared he would become. Politically, I felt overrun and, more so, that my home had become stuck in the worst version of itself. I wanted to be part of fixing that brokenness, and I thought repair could start in our little corner of Pennsylvania. Or, at least, I could start there.

"So, I ask you: Are you as angry at Congress, at your state legislature, at your party—at everyone—as I am? Are you afraid? Are you burnt out?" Amanda Litman writes in *Don't Just March, Run for Something*. "Forget about Congress, though," Litman writes. "Focus on the offices that actually get shit done—state legislatures, city councils, school boards, and mayorships. Look at who's leading the resistance: the local officials who truly understand their communities."

In 2018, I decided to give it a try. I figured I was bright and friendly enough to break through the local GOP wall. Specifically, I planned to run for the Pennsylvania state house of representatives against a long-term incumbent I considered particularly feckless. He practices a political style that favors anger-baiting social media posts, targeting the usual punching bags: Democrats, teachers, immigrants, and members of the LGBTQ+ community. I had two years to get ramped up for 2020, when I'd take a shot at his seat in PA House District 6.

* * *

Let's get this out of the way: I lost.

And when I say *lost*, I mean that in the 2020 election, I got less than 35 percent of the vote across the two-county district. Almost 10,000—9,999 to be exact—fewer people voted for me than for the low-effort, low-idea Republican incumbent, who scooped up the most votes in his career and enjoyed the widest margin of victory in his career. A small consolation, I suppose, is that I outperformed all of the top-of-ticket Democrats, including Joe Biden. But I still got shellacked, badly.

This is a familiar story in rural America. Registration deficits are so bad that Democrats are essentially guaranteed losers. The state Democratic Party agrees, so it spends its time and cash on races that spreadsheets indicate are worthwhile, where margins of victory overwhelmingly favor Democrats or are at least close. As a result, the party favors urban and suburban districts, ones with Democratic registration majorities or toss-up races. Rural counties just don't have enough Democrats, and the state party's disinterest filters down to the county party and leads to typically weak turnout among both voters and candidates.

Something I learned as a candidate: Political parties care mostly, if not entirely, about winning elections. That might seem obvious, but the distinction is crucial. Parties do not particularly care about governance, and are disinterested in spending any time or money trying to reach voters in places where they historically lose. That means political parties function always within the scope of numerical binaries. Win versus loss. If a place fits neatly in the loss column, then a political party won't be interested in spending resources there.

When we hear words like "gerrymander," we understand it signifies something untoward. We usually think about how it is deployed by whichever party we consider our antithesis, and we get angry about how the deck is stacked unfairly. In reality, legislative gerrymandering is the effective raison d'être of both the GOP and DNC as a means to solidify as many "safe" districts as possible. While groups interested in democratic progress and fairness believe, as do I, that we're all better off when elections are competitive, political parties disagree. They just want to win. And since elected politicians literally write the rules of their own elections, an astonishingly small number of elections wind up being competitive on election night, particularly at the state level. If you happen to be one of the many Americans who lives in a place with a lopsided partisan registration split, you also know which party will bother investing in local campaigning and which won't. More and more of us live in places with lopsided splits these days.

One of the dispiriting effects of running for office was learning the difference between civic myth and the reality of elections. When I started as a candidate, I still believed in the spirit of the attempt, was convinced that showing energy and ideas could draw support from the state party, win over voters, and help me pull off the upset. I still believed in the capacity of political change. I still believed in the civic rhetoric we learn in school, an appealing notion of fair play and responsibility. I still believed that when people say they are tired of partisan arguments and just want good people doing the work of government, they mean it. I still believed them when they say, "I vote person over party."

These are lies most voters tell themselves before they go and pull the lever, almost always, for whichever party they have landed in through principle or happenstance. Political scientists have studied the thorny problem of partisan rigidity, and they have found that candidates have almost no capacity to shift partisan fidelity during elections. Best case, a candidate can shift an election a percent or two relative to registration splits, and even that requires enormous effort and expense. This is why the hardest work of political bodies focuses on voter suppression, party registration, and ever more sophisticated models of gerrymandering. Ideas and debate don't win elections. Registration splits do.

This is American politics in a nutshell, where the sophistication of electoral machinations has established a system where politics shapes voting blocks, instead of people shaping political action. Districts are gerrymandered into one party control. Issues are reduced to marketing slogans by national advertising. Parties become shorthand identities that feel real even though they are technically voluntary and essentially irrelevant to most of our daily lives. All of this works out nicely for politicians, of course, because it makes campaigns easy.

For actual people, however, this dynamic creates a troubling, very real, and effective disenfranchisement. The almost 10,000 people who voted for me, for example, do not, in some real sense, exist politically. Our incumbent rep has said, specifically, this on multiple occasions, explaining that he makes policy decisions simply by voting the way he thinks the majority of Crawford County residents would vote. He practices a familiar political style that serves as the very definition of pandering. A truly engaged and ethical elected official would weigh the evidence of policy effectiveness, instead of merely following the easiest winds of local vibes. In a recent local op-ed, he spent a surprising number of words repeating the phrase "you matter" while also writing that anyone outside of the local Republican majority will probably think they don't matter because he will never cast votes in Harrisburg that align with their values. So, while you matter, what you think does not. And I don't need to tell you that, in reality, you also don't matter to a politician like him if you don't think and vote the way he does.

* * *

That I lost is all I really have to say about my campaign itself because what is there really to say? How do I tell this story in a way that doesn't make you think you have heard it before?

I mean, really, how do I write a story about loss in a way that matters, to you, in any way other than strategic? Because even in progressive circles, not mattering is the fate of rural Americans. You don't hear many national progressives referencing rural America and asking, *How do we win there?* Sometimes they get behind the idea of losing a little less badly. But most of the time they just wonder how they can cancel out rural losses by running up margins of victory in urban areas.

I am writing about our losses, which is directly about my failed election, but also about how the GOP's domination of rural politics is really about you, wherever you live, and also about how the Democratic Party's abandonment of rural geographies is also about you, wherever you live. More importantly, I am writing about how we all lose when politics separates itself from the substance of real lives, when being part of a group of 10,000 means both that your values get walloped in every election and that the party that performatively allies itself to you will do nothing to stop the walloping. I am writing about being given up on, which is the fate of those of us who live in places like where I live. Economically. Politically. Culturally.

We pay the price of abandonment in rural America. I want you to understand that you pay those prices even if you don't live here, or think about here, or actually care about here. The easiest thing to do is ignore rural Americans, or make jokes about us, or hate us for delivering the bullshit politicians we deliver to state and federal legislatures. Ignoring, hating, and ridiculing us is, of course, how the bullshit politicians stay in power. As a nation, we aren't going to get anything other than what we've been getting until we recognize a hard, painful truth that I hope you can hear as a call to action, and not just as another installment of rural literary cliché. The ragged rough bullshit politics of rural America delineate our abandonment and its costs.

* * *

When I was just getting started with all this, in the quieter parts of the early campaign, I met with a retired colleague active in local progressive politics. We sipped coffee in the campus center while sharing the general shit-talking that forges partisan bonds: how bad the current dude was, how politics are broken, this and that.

"So why do you want to run?" he asked me, rather suddenly.

I remember being stumped for a moment, which struck me as a problem. I mean, isn't this the most fundamental question of every candidacy? Yet it's also the one that often seems murkiest. Why does anyone run, or want to run, or be an elected official, or in general seek the kind of tainted quasi-powerful position of continual disappointment that is politics? At least for me, wanting to run was based on an inkling of desire, of knowing things could be better than they are.

In the moment, I answered by slipping back into issues. Health care. Environment. Education. The big three of my platform, each of which ran contrary to local conservative dogma but which I thought could actually create meaningful positive local change. I still think that, in fact. Rural areas suffer diminishment in all of these areas with negative effects on quality of life and general prosperity.

But I hadn't yet learned that elections are not really about issues. Not even the big elections. The big three of my platform signaled me as *progressive*, which more than a few "open-minded" conservative voters took the time to point out by sending me hateful messages during the campaign. What I also hadn't yet learned was that my progressive colleague voted for me, but supported my candidacy only slightly more than the right wingers who sent me hate mail. I "earned" his vote because I was a Democrat, not because he believed in me or my chances. In fact, later in the campaign he emailed everyone in the local progressive organization to urge them to donate money to candidates in Pittsburgh because, he wrote, there was no one on the ballot in Crawford County who could feasibly win. You can't win elections in rural places when even your progressive supporters see progressive candidacy as hopeless.

* * *

When I sat with the County Democratic Chair in 2018, I sat directly across Meadville's downtown Diamond Park, where a historical marker seemed to mock me. The form of primary election used in most of America was invented right here in Crawford County, by the Democratic Party, way back in 1842. They started nominating elections largely because of intraparty fighting that handed a gubernatorial win to Joseph Rittner in 1835, a member of the Anti-Masonic Party, who carried what was then heavily Democratic Crawford County because Democrats siphoned votes from each another instead of maintaining party unity. That's to say, the direct primary was invented less as an exercise in fairness and more to guarantee that a third-party candidate like Rittner couldn't sneak up and seize control. This is an important aspect of primary elections we need to understand. They were invented by one of the major American political parties, and they are maintained through a coalition of the two major parties largely to prevent any other parties from gaining traction. Primaries are, in a sense, a way to rig the dice for the parties.

By 1856, however, Democrats didn't matter at all in Crawford County. That's the year John Frémont became the first Republican nominee for president, carrying the county even as he lost the election to James Buchanan, who was from Pennsylvania and whose sister actually lived in Meadville. Since that election, only three Democratic presidential candidates have ever carried Crawford County: LBJ in 1964, when he destroyed then-unelectable Barry Goldwater; Woodrow Wilson in 1916, when he squeaked out a win over Charles Evan Hughes; and William Jennings Bryan in 1896, when he lost for the first of two successive campaigns to

Progressive Republican William McKinley. McKinley, as it so happens, had been a student at Allegheny College, where I teach, and I sometimes wonder if the long-standing local suspicion of "college people" factored into his loss.

More broadly, in the last fifty years, only two Democrats have held a seat in the state house for any of the county's three districts. That means Democrats have held a grand total of six two-year sessions in the area's aggregate seventy-five. There hasn't been a Democratic state senator since the 1930s. And if you count up all the votes from all the elections at all levels of government since 1900, 60 percent of them have gone to Republicans. I'm sure you can guess the percentage of Crawford County voters registered as Republicans. I'm sure you can guess why I lost my election even before I started.

* * *

"So why do you want to run?"

Looking back, I recognize that I ran for office for deeply personal reasons, related to home and region and identity. I ran because neither my progressive colleague nor the hate-mailers see validity in rural progressive identity. This is, perhaps obviously, the problem. So few people are willing to see the hope present in different conceptions of what it means to be rural. Far too many limit the politics of "red states" through stereotype and the constant repetition of trope.

I ran for office because my political desire is rooted in beauty and peace. These are the core tenets of life, in my view. They are the underlying principles, I believe, even of our Constitution if you read it carefully. Beauty and peace, however, are not winning political strategies.

* * *

Back to the start, to Democratic HQ, to the end of my meeting with the county Chair. She and I stood on the front porch beneath the vinyl flag, under the donkey. She lit a cigarette, took a drag. A cold rain started again. It was only five o'clock but the gloomy night seemed to have been around forever.

"Do you think you want to be part of our team?" she asked me.

I wasn't actually sure, but I figured I could try. I might not fit exactly, but at least I could try to fashion a fit. What does fitting in ever really look like around here for someone like me, with the Crawford Democrats or, to be honest, the Democrat Party writ large, or possibly with Crawford County at all?

"Yes," I said.

Leaves rattled in the gutters. The sky would dump a foot of snow overnight. My phone buzzed, a friend texting. "The coast is clear," meaning the French class my wife was teaching at our house had ended. Our families were having pizza together, a Friday routine. I had normal life things to do, once I finished with the politics.

"My landlord laughs at me," the Chair said. "'Why don't you just smoke inside,' he asks? But I always go outside."

Her demeanor moved toward the melancholy, and I remember a deep sadness in her posture. She wished more people would use HQ. She told me that's why she pays for Wi-Fi and cable even though money is short. She wanted noise in the HQ so it wouldn't feel so empty. She wondered if college students were afraid of her. They show up once and never return, she told me. She seemed to long for the party itself, for a collection of people who shared common purpose and whose lively human contact matters.

I wonder now if she hoped, like me, for a sign that being a rural Democrat is more than a lonely fate of political irrelevance. It isn't easy being a rural Democrat. It isn't easy being alone. It isn't easy being the one who has to represent Democrats in election after election, and see the ship constantly take on water.

As I got ready to head home, she paused and drew in smoke. She exhaled.

"Have you considered running as a Republican?" she asked me.

I don't know whether this was meant as a strategic plan, or as a test, or just as a random comment tossed into the chilling air. But it carried sorrow and truth, the recognition that the easiest way to win is to play the game the way the rules are rigged.

And what can you say, really? About the ancient values dormant in the label "Republican." About the great tragedy of ideological erosion that has led us to where we are. About how being a Democrat often feels simply being not something else.

No, I said. I knew that, at least.

This might be the real moment I lost the election. There would have been time to register as a Republican, and most voters pay so little attention to local races I might have been able to pull it off. I might have been able to fashion a message that would have won the primary. I don't know.

Well, actually, I do. I lived through 2020 and so did you. I would not have won the Republican primary because no decent person could. Trying to do so might have actually been dangerous.

The Chair nodded. She took a final pull on her cigarette, tossed it to the ground, and snuffed it into the concrete with her heel. I was the candidate now, in all ways but the paperwork I would soon file. It was time to get on with the losing, to have the results of the election pose the same question I ask myself over and over again: Do I even belong here at all?

Well, I refuse to accept that I come from a place that cannot be redeemed. I think that matters. I think it still matters, loss notwithstanding.

★ **TWO** ★

I HATE IT HERE, PLEASE VOTE FOR ME

As you approach the rise of Meadville's Smock Bridge, the unfurled machismo of a ginormous American flag more or less marks the line between Vernon Township and the city itself. Vernon officially calls itself the "Golden Link" of Crawford County, "link" describing a loose confederation of Walmart, strip plazas, car dealerships and, most importantly, taxes far lower than those within the city limits. Just like so many places in the formerly industrial northeast, even the businesses and residents who have stuck around continue decamping from the municipal center to cut costs.

The giant flag at this point of demarcation belongs to one of the biggest manufacturers still left in Crawford County, a maker of now-ubiquitous adjustable pliers invented here in the 1930s.

You probably have a pair in your toolbox, or your junk drawer, or at least have a knockoff design. They're good pliers, genius really. The pliers transformed a company that started off making farrier's tools, then general hardware, into a brand that defines a category. Like Kleenex, but for tools: Channellock.

Their supersized flag is pretty new, though. It replaced a sober-scale version shortly after the election of Donald Trump in 2016, which might be a coincidence, but I've seen the political donation records. The owner of the company is one of the biggest GOP donors in the region. Based on the fashion of Crawford County's rightward lean, I doubt "coincidental" is the right word to use. The flag was hoisted almost assuredly as a symbol of a swath of America thrilled with both the outcome of the 2016 election and the sorrows many others felt afterward.

As a result, every time I pass that flag, I can't help but see an implied message. Something about dominion, muscularity, and finger-flipping, all of it not a ton different from the effect of driving back roads in the county and seeing variations of Trump signs that have remained steadfast for going on seven years now, well into the middle of the succeeding presidency. The message of the whopper flag beside Smock Bridge appears to me like a riff on the company's marketing slogan: "Born here. Made here. Staying here." It reads as aggressive, whether intended to or not, because of the way words carry layers of history.

Here. That word. I think about it a lot these days, probably always have. One of my primary artistic preoccupations has been the triangulation of identity and geography, how our place in the world shapes us in mysterious ways. In politics, *here* falls into the category of weaponized shorthand, a shifty concept nonetheless terribly useful for cleaving electorates into camps. Stories of nativity have outsized influence in politics, a perpetual contradiction of the ethos of America as a land of reinvention and immigrant pride, which has always been simultaneously true and absolutely not.

Where you are *from* winds up mattering for a political candidate in nonsensical, always contradictory, but thoroughly impactful ways. As a candidate I learned, for example, the power of pointing out your family's "original" presence in your region. Mostly, I learned that I was unable to make that claim in Crawford County, and the absence of that claim mattered to many voters. *Original* is also a shifty word, of course, because the starting point of a geographical clock shapes itself to whatever imagined moment fits the desires of those who have established and maintain dominion. *Original* erases the history of the actual originals, defines the set-point of located history as the moment a place was conquered, as defined by those who did the conquering. This, too, is America in a nutshell.

I grew up two hours away from Meadville, in the same state, in a town with a functionally identical industrial history and similar contemporary economic struggle. Still, I was an outsider candidate because I could not evoke the "born here" part of a marketing slogan. The dude I ran against sent out a campaign flier that fixated on that simple comment. He invoked his deep locality by listing the name of the church where he was baptized, and the name of the one where he was married, and the names of his grandparents. The big gotcha was the line about me, pointing out that I had only lived in the region for ten years. Not enough, politically.

The flier was dumb. You need to understand that. It was shoddy, grammatically awkward, and badly designed. Cheap. But it spoke to a political reality you hear time and again in local politics: Only "natives" have claim to office. This was an attack I had anticipated, though. From the start of my campaign, I had sought to point out the similarities of my nearby birthplace and my current residence. *Two hours* became the phrase, at least in my mind. I grew up *only two hours* away in a place exactly like this one. *Two hours* designated closeness, to here and to the people of here. In two hours, you can walk five or six miles, and that's not far at all.

A problem, however, is that two hours is also a term of escape, because Meadville is also *just two hours* from Pittsburgh or Cleveland or Buffalo, the *just* in this syntax deployed by people who live *here* but wish they did not. Many who wind up here for professional reasons, maybe to work at the medical center or at the College, aren't completely sold on the region where their lives have become rooted. For them, *two hours* is a sigh of relief or a prayer of deliverance. Two hours is not far, thank god, just a quick trip to somewhere with a *real* culture.

And I get it. Moving into rural areas can feel alienating, even dangerous, particularly when public rhetoric tends to identify longtime residents as disqualified if they were not *born here*, even if they are *staying here*. Like many college towns, a false distinction holds sway between local residents and "college people." Many of the latter have lived here longer than the "locals," but that's beside the point. Certainly, the sense of difference is not universal, as plenty of people move here and commit, just as many whose families have long been here are keen to welcome the constant evolution of neighborliness.

Yet the understanding of who is *really from here* lies always just under the surface. It's the kind of wound that pops out in moments of frustration or disgust. In recent elections for city council and school board, Meadville "locals" have made aggressive attacks on both the College and the people who work there, because to them the College is not *from here*. Such people define everything associated with the College as foreign to Meadville, blame the College for its presence, even bizarrely argue the town would be better off without its anchor institution at all. Notably, the College was actually founded before the city was chartered, but that's beside the point.

Here versus *there* has bearing even as it holds no stable meaning. Similarly, *two hours* carries both distance and proximity, signaling that I grew up nearby and quite far away, *just two hours* away and a *whole two hours* away. Time and distance travelled are a symbolic measurement of both and neither. Liminal, to use an academic's cliché. In the end, I am nothing, because two hours is both too close and too far, and that's the sticking point of my life as much as for my election. I am somehow always an outsider. I am too local and too foreign, all at once. It just depends on who is measuring the distance. And *two hours*, as in how far away I was born, meant I was effectively from the other side of the planet, and somehow also too parochial. Audience matters, as always, in politics.

That said, Channellock is, indeed, part of *here*, and has been *fiercely made*, to borrow from their marketing schlock again, in the shop next to the railroad tracks over which the Smock Bridge stretches. It's a union place, which is good, but with a union vibe *fiercely made* in the image of a new kind of labor deal, one that sees owners and workers all voting the same right-leaning way, and all with a mutual agreement that decent wages *for here* are good enough, particularly as long as no one else in town offers greater ones. Wages *for here*, in general, are very low, something the people paying those low wages like to describe as a "low cost of living." A whispered local story describes a moment fifteen or twenty years ago when a big multinational beer company wanted to set up shop in Meadville. The local industrial leaders found a way to block it because they worried about how that arrival would apply upward pressure to their own stagnated wage structures.

Maybe the story is true, maybe not. It's true enough in practice, because one local business leader wrote an op-ed not that long ago about how ridiculous it would be to raise the state minimum wage from $7.25, as that would just force local business owners to give more of *their money* to workers. He made it clear that all of the revenues of a company belong to the owner, who should be applauded for giving any of it to workers, because he argues that paying wages for work is essentially an act of benevolence. Higher wages might be fine for other places, he argued, but it would just punish people like him, who have made their living based on the depressed economic landscape of Rust Belt abandonment.

The Rust Belt, I think it is safe to say, can lay claim to locality: *Born here. Made here. Staying here.*

* * *

From the top of the family farm, you can see the hospital where I was born, and the tower of Indiana University of Pennsylvania's John Sutton Hall, the golden dome of the old Indiana County Courthouse, and a few iconic white church spires poking out of the green landscape of northern Appalachia. You can see a series of radio towers atop the hills, which are in fact the highest remnants of the Appalachian Plateau that has eroded into what we call mountains.

You can also see the churning stacks of the Homer City Generating Station, a coal-fired plant often ranked as one of the most polluting in the country. The power plant is a little cleaner than it used to be, thanks to expensive scrubbers in the stacks, but it still isn't churning out clean air. Every day, white vapor rolls into the sky from fat cooling towers, artificial clouds carrying mercury, sulfur dioxide, and nitrogen dioxide. High voltage power lines bisect the top of the family farm, running straight to the distant power plant. Every couple of years, crews show up to maintain the right of way, which means they squirt weed killer and hack down sprouted trees with a brush hog. A few years ago, they felled a few century cherry trees, leaving the wood to rot. All for the power plant.

"What I come from made me who I am," Janisse Ray writes in *Ecology of a Cracker Childhood*, a memoir of her sense of self in relationship to the flat leaf pines of Georgia, of a regional

environmental legacy built on clear-cutting, and on her own
early years growing up in a junkyard. It's a remarkable book of
reconciliation. Ray comes to own her sense of place as a way of
speaking to the complexity of her particular Southern, ecosensi-
tive sense.

So it is for me, reckoning always the many layers of my childhood on a southwestern Pennsylvania farm and my adult life in
a Rust Belt city roughened by the loss of its manufacturing industry. It's fair to say that roaming across the depleted fields of the
family farm, wading mine-tainted creeks, and watching winter
snow turn black from strip mine coal dust, made me a political
candidate. How could it not?

I grew up with a father committed to deep family roots in
Pennsylvania, with a grandfather who drove giant shovels in the
anthracite fields of the eastern part of the state, and a mother
who often lamented the industrial violence that contributed to
the demise of her hometown of Gary, Indiana. I grew up, also,
with parents who committed themselves to a life of quiet restoration, the family farm as a site of embedded devotion. To their
dreams. To their children. To a holy stewardship of land that
each always viewed, I imagine, through the lens of their
Lutheran-Catholic, theologically mixed marriage.

Their restoration began by buying the farm out of bankruptcy, from a contractor who had planned to build a suburban-
style subdivision atop the slip shale. My parents set to clearing
choking weeds. Stubborn poison ivy thickets inspired them to
buy their first goat, an Alpine my sister named Edelweiss. The
goat spent many days happily munching away at the poison ivy.

Renovating a dilapidated farmhouse came next. It was worth so little that their insurance agent would only write a policy based on the collateral of the weathered barn. My parents read Wendell Berry and Aldo Leopold, and the farm became an experiment in the mysteries of reclamation, spiritual and otherwise.

I grew up walking the hills of this southwestern Pennsylvania farm, sometimes as a nascent writer and sometimes with a rifle, hunting deer or groundhogs. I grew up as a musician, and a theater kid, and an AP kid, and a 4-H kid. The point is that I see no contradiction in these identities. My parents were teachers and farmers, working class kids who were the first in their families to attend college. I grew up in a world that included the sort of rural expansiveness that I know is endemic to many, where the divide is not between the arts and economy, or between insiders and outsiders, or between families long-rooted in the local dirt and newcomers to be shunned, or even between what has been lost and what can be restored. At the risk of sounding optimistic, my rural childhood made a case for rural vitality and open horizons.

Rural America thrives when we recognize these tensions. It languishes when we don't. Rural America could thrive if it resisted the siren song of "again," which is a nostalgia rooted in false senses of prosperity and false destinies of decline. The slow work of restoration is a deeply embedded politics, manifesting as a love of place instead of as a love of party.

* * *

A local moniker for Meadville is "Tool City," a relatively recent label applied when small-scale tool and die shops proliferated as an outgrowth of the major local industry, the zipper. Meadville happens to be the birthplace of the American zipper, and a large percentage of residents worked for Talon, which was kicking serious zipper ass through the 1960s as the world's dominant manufacturer.

Recently, I discovered that my dad's old Kutztown State College windbreaker, circa 1959, had a Talon Zipper. I posted a picture on Facebook, and a local friend reposted it with a brief sad lament about his own father working there, and the loss of his job, and the general melancholic echo of this centerpiece of Meadville work. Because, yes, Talon is one of those stories. The company entered the phase of corporate takeovers in the 1960s, just as competition from foreign zipper makers was ramping up. The company starting losing money, and it started moving operations to Mexico, and by the 1990s Talon was gone from Meadville.

The company left an abandoned building, which Crawford County eventually bought, then razed for a hefty sum, and then had to spend more to clean up tainted soil. That cleared the way for a discount cheap-build apartment speculator to arrive, thanks to a big tax-abatement deal from the county. The apartments were built, and rented to senior citizens, who in 2022 took it on the nose when the company announced rent hikes of 35 percent.

That's an unfortunately familiar tale of abandonment and cost, literal and emotional. You see it all the time in the parts of America that suffer economically. And we've seen it over and over again here in Crawford County. We pay for our own abandonment in so many ways. Companies make a fortune, then hop town. The people left behind in the gutted place have to find ways to both fill the void of loss and pay to clean up messes invariably left behind.

Before Talon, American Viscose started churning out rayon in the 1920s, employing many in Meadville. In the 1980s, the company offered a wage-slashing contract to the workers: The workers said that wasn't fair; the company fired pretty much everyone in 1985. Two weeks later, an infamous tornado swarm killed eleven in the county and close to one hundred in the tri-state area.

Before American Viscose, the Spirella Company mastered the corset in the early twentieth century, birthing a massive international company that anchored Meadville to the world. But corsets went out of fashion, and long before that Spirella had shifted itself to London.

Before and during all of this, locomotives used to be repaired down by French Creek, and local legend brags of Meadville as the midway rail stop between Chicago and New York. We had two opera houses, people say. The Great Depression didn't even make a ripple here, they say. We used to be something, they say. Weren't we something? We really used to be something.

Used to is the dire slogan that defines us. Over on Arch Street, where the Talon Zipper factory used to be. Down in the 5th Ward, along the flood-prone banks of French Creek, where the American Viscose Factory used to be. Over on Chestnut Street, where the old Unitarian seminary used to be. On French Creek, where an oil absorption boom perpetually floats to stem the permanent oil seep left behind by the rail shop that used to be there. The school that used to be open. The restaurant you used to love. The prosperity that used to be here.

Things got bad gradually then suddenly, as Hemingway might put it. Meadville peaked in the middle of the twentieth century with just shy of 15,000 residents. As of the 2020 census, there were only 12,000 people left. Our economy is among the worst in the state of Pennsylvania, with Crawford County ranking fifty-sixth out of the state's sixty-seven counties in per capita income. One in four residents of Meadville lives below the poverty line.

All of that, I think, is carried in the symbolism of the flag beside the Smock Bridge. And, credit to Channellock, they are still here, one of the few. That deserves recognition and respect. Yet so much is no longer here, a reason we cling to what remains. And claims to *staying here* carry a bitterness because of what has not stayed, and because of how the politics of those in control of the staying perpetuate the decline. And because of who is allowed to stay, or allowed to count at all as being local. And because even this company, the one that stays, stays because it has shaped this place into what it wants it to be, fierce perhaps, but fierce only in the way it wishes the place to be fierce, fierce in preventing the unfurling blooms of what so many desire and need and find trampled or battered by their perpetual isolation and exile.

* * *

Lost is the word that rattles around in my head. So much has been lost. So much continues to be lost. Loss is our present, active, ongoing, repeating unbroken active verb.

I lost an election, to the physical embodiment of mediocre white dude conservatism. We are losing our shared sense of civic democracy. We have lost an economy. Our rural politics have been consumed by resentment and ire. I don't want to live in a place animated by hatred and smallness, a place that languishes in economic collapse, a place that prizes its past, but fears its future, that hates even itself. So I ran for office with the hope that we can be better than we've been. Yet I lost, badly.

I want to reconcile this place and my life, but the politics of my home feel like a banishment. More than anything, I want to be able to sit on a farmhouse porch in western Pennsylvania, listen to night insects sing as the hills recede into the darkness, and know we deserve that beauty.

I long for the nighttime horizon of the family farm, where the blinking warning lights of the generating station gleam. I have to admit I see them as beautiful because, well, that's part of being from a place like this. It's part of loving the things that harm you, part of the pull of things that cause the harm. Even when you know things are bad for you, it's hard to quit them, sometimes because you love it too much to risk leaving, sometimes because you love it too much to stay. Sometimes you love it so much you run for office, which is a different way of staying and going, of winning and losing somehow all at once.

The greatest insult is that I am cast as a stranger in my own home. Literally, in the case of my election, but also generally, by everyone everywhere, it seems. I ran to try, to reach out to my unwelcoming home and call it my home. I ran to change the dynamic of perpetual loss, to be part of saving and fixing what has become so deeply broken.

I am a political stranger in my own home, just as rural Americans have been made to feel strangers to the politics of the American left. Obama and Clinton each offered spectacular reinforcement of that exile, misunderstanding their own embrace of rural disdain. What they saw were rednecks and hillbillies clinging to their guns. They saw baskets of deplorables.

Except that Obama and Clinton were also not wrong, not really. It's possible they miscalculated the impact of their comments, and I am certain their criticism reveals their lack of strategic concern for the daily experience of those excluded from the dark monotone of rural conservative caricature but, who nonetheless, are *from here*. Yet the political reality of places like Crawford County mean its elections are dominated by the caricatures of rural trope. How we vote can be described as nothing other than deplorable.

Nonetheless, rural Americans are not wrong to feel disrespected. Being rural means you're underestimated, just like everyone who lives in the wreckage of neoliberal capitalism is underestimated. We hear the stories of being overlooked by the loud-shouting right wingers, the ones who took offense to Obama and Clinton. We don't hear the stories of the others who are overlooked. The small Black population of Meadville, whose ancestors fought to create the first integrated primary school in Pennsylvania, all the way back in 1881. Those in the LGBTQ+ community who refuse to be intimidated by area school boards leading the charge to ban books as a way to ban identities. The doctors, faculty, and students who come to Meadville with all manner of ethnic, racial, and gender identities and make a home here, some for four years some forever.

I think, now, of the people who came to the few in-person campaign events I was able to hold, a couple early in the campaign and a couple late in the summer of 2020 once we all learned at least some ways to manage Covid. Each of these spaces was filled with people erased in stories of monolithic rural America: Muslim, Jewish, actually progressive Christian, Black and Asian-American and Latinx, gay, straight and trans, rich doctors and struggling cashiers, all of them coming together to show a different image of *here*. In each of these spaces, I found support and connection with the ribbon of folks who care about the way so many of us share wounds. Some of those are economic, for sure. Some are the consequence of industrial abandonment. Many are the bruises of unchallenged domination by the most virulent strains of rabid conservatism, those who are drawn to the incendiary rhetoric of Trumpism. Sixty against forty, alas, signals the way the virulent control our political fate, very much by denying membership to the community they fashion in their own image.

Politics cares little about human value. Politics cares little, even, about the hole Talon Zipper left in the heart of our local economy. Politics is about leveraging such stories to perpetuate the scam of weaponized partisan bullshittery. The collapse of an economy is good for politics, because politicians get to use it as an example of how the other side has failed, even though no side actually cares that much unless caring can be measured in votes.

All of this is to say *being from here* actually is a valid concern. It's just that defining who and what counts as local is more than a little screwed up. You can be *from here* all your life, and it doesn't count. Not if who you are doesn't fit the easy sketch of what *here* supposedly is.

* * *

I want to live in a place I love. Don't we all? I want to live in a place that loves me, too.

One of the harder truths of my candidacy was that I should have lost, at least if we think a representative should be a snapshot of dominant local values instead of a public servant working to make their community better. I ran wanting to win, and wanting to build this place into a different kind of home, less reflective of where I came from and more about where I want to be from. I ran because I hate living in a place like this, which means I was running not to represent the region but to transform it into something it could be. The place, however, saw little reason to want change.

I learned that at least this part of rural America seems happy with the self it has allowed itself to become and is not ashamed of its violence, hatred, and exclusion. I can argue this place has lost itself to destructive forces, but the self I imagine for my home might be an invention or a dream. Rural America might not wish to be changed. Because of that, it is hard to know if I can be from here any longer, if I can stay.

Here lies the problem of running for office as the member of an oppositional party: You run because you think things could be better, because you refuse to carry water for the lies of the political narratives that distort the reality of your jurisdiction. You run for office because you want to change things, which is to say you run because you recognize that things are *not good* or at least not as good as they could be. That's an insult to the thinly aware, and it is a threat to the deep-pocketed czars of small town rural places who can own politicians by donating rather small sums of money to their campaigns. Either way, this dynamic is continually reinforced by a social hierarchy that begins by separating who is from here and who is not, and is then further clarified by who gets to decide what here needs and what it doesn't.

* * *

I have a complicated and uneasy relationship with my home state, and an even more troubled one with the part of Pennsylvania that has become our home. My wife, Jen, and I moved here in 2011, relocating *only two hours* from my hometown, and two-and-a-half from hers. Prior to that, we spent seven years in the Laurel Mountains of southwestern Pennsylvania, our happy landing spot after moving back after a year living in Paris, and before that four in the high desert of southeastern Arizona. The Laurel Mountains felt like home, a resettling into our childhood mountains. We dug in, bought a house, had our first child, were glad to live close to our parents, imagined a life of proximity to family.

Maybe our story is inevitable for the sorts of places we're from: Jen lost her job teaching primary and middle school French because the school decided French didn't matter anymore. I was passed over for a permanent teaching job at my university alma mater, where I had been working. I was too local, a faculty brat townie who earned his B.A. from that very department. The circumstances of fading economies, essentially, created a forced departure, even if our stories were told with academic overtones instead of industrial ones. There was no work for us to make a life where our life felt most settled. We were lucky, though, and landed well when I was hired at Allegheny College, *only two hours away*, in a place close to home but clearly not quite.

I admit I am fussy about concepts of place. Essentially, I echo what Scott Russell Sanders writes about his Ohio birthplace, that I instinctively measure the arc of landscapes using the family farm as a baseline. There, the hills are steep, which makes northwestern Pennsylvania seem uncomfortably flat by my standards. A lot of that is the effect of glaciation, which flattened out this part of the Appalachian Plateau but stopped before scouring places farther south. This matters to me, probably more than it should.

More crucially, the far upper-left corner of the state feels different culturally. I joke sometimes that it's the Ohio part of Pennsylvania, and sometimes that seems exactly right. There's an altered tone of industrial loss, which I recognize as a weird baseline for defining a concept of home. But so it is. Which is perhaps one of the things hardest to understand about places where things have gone badly if you're not from one. Our own romantic notions of home are tied up in the way it has been roughened. Still, it seems to matter. In northwestern Pennsylvania, the lost industries were in manufacturing, while the industries that abandoned Jen's hometown and my own were steel and coal. While you might think absence is absence, the residue of those cultural histories just cuts differently.

The contrast boils down essentially to a distinction between Rust Belt and Appalachia, which probably relates most directly to industrial earthiness. I come from a place where the industry was pulled from the earth itself; where I live now is a place that made and assembled objects. All of this affects me in ways that have made Meadville feel like a provisional home for more than a decade now, even if Meadville isn't all that different at heart from my hometown. I always feel disoriented here, dizzy, but also guilty that I don't love it.

I have reasons for my ambivalence, or excuses. The easy one is that I learned I had a brain tumor here. It's hard to have affection for a place you associate with your own mortality. Worse, I sometimes blame the condition on our locally infamous water system, or on the decaying condition of the building where I work, where half a dozen of the twenty-five or so who work there have been diagnosed with tumors. Whatever the cause, Meadville is the place where I lay in bed for months recovering from surgery and radiation, where I watched Brexit happen while recovering, where later in the year I gaped at the television as Trump won the presidency. These associations make little sense outside of my own mind, but they matter to me as part of the texture of *here*. I will always carry a visceral association of my embodied struggle and the currency of the rise of right-wing demagoguery with my sense of this place.

Northwestern Pennsylvania also feels like a time warp, sometimes in good ways but often not. Among the bad is the way a
small cabal of conservative "civic leaders" call the shots, and these
leaders are all *from here*, and they know it, and they know who
isn't, and I am not, nor is anyone who moves to Meadville to
work at the College or at the medical center.

Of course, to undermine myself, the politics of *here* are no
different from the politics of my hometown, whether you
measure it in party registration, election outcomes, or the general arc of local conversations. Both places have been Republican pretty much forever, and both have suffered the co-optation
of traditional Republican values by ever-deepening collapses into
right-wing impulses. Both places are culturally dominated by the
gruff rumblings of rural machismo, the driving force of contemporary rural politics. Both places growl at you if you dare
criticize the way things are. Love it or leave it, etc.

You already understand the surface politics of *here* with the
usual punch list, which, as it turns out, is also literally the
unchanging platform of the politician I failed to unseat. Taxes
are bad. Guns are good. Abortions should be illegal. Circulat-
ing underneath that surface "conservatism" is a poisoned root
system of fear, resentment, anger, struggle, violence, weariness.

This is precisely why rural politics matters: While the urges
of the right wing have seized control of my home landscapes, the
strategic mastery of the contemporary GOP has figured out how
to increase the death spiral gravitational pull of rural America as
the black hole of MAGA bullshit. I want to say that's a surprise,
but I've lived my entire life in the bosom of rural right-wing

extremism. I have witnessed the GOP's rural strategy execute a veer from the investments of Eisenhower to the dog-whistling economic destruction of Reagan to the rabid foam-mouthed violence of Trumpism. For my entire life, home has been a place of decay and abandonment.

I've grown so tired of living in such places, and that might be the simplest explanation for the voice in my head that encouraged me to step into the political world. The ideas that hold us captive have been too often unchallenged, which is also a way to say that many of the people who live *here* are utterly erased by the dominance of right-wing rural narratives. In terms of an election, a sixty-five to thirty-five shellacking functions as a binary one versus zero, particularly when the aggregate outcome of every election since the earth's crust cooled, it seems, has had the same outcome. That's why the election maps color Crawford and Indiana counties in deep red.

But that thirty-five is also *here*, and has always been *here*, even though it gets no credit for being here. Locally, your vote doesn't really matter, because you get whipped every time. Nationally, your existence doesn't matter, because the color on the election map is all anyone sees. The consequences of that political erasure are immense. Consider the clichés of rural spaces: white, straight, at least a little racist, undereducated, working class, Republican. Yet two of the largest employers in Crawford County are the hospital and the college where I teach. More broadly, even within just the confines of PA House District 6, you find the breadth of American diversity, in race, gender, sexuality, nationality, and income. The district has an international (water) border with

Canada, farmland in the middle, a formerly industrial small city as the epicenter, bottom-of-the-heap per capita income in that city and affluent suburbs up by Lake Erie. All of that is washed away with a simple mathematical shorthand: 60 > 40.

Rural politics don't have to be this way, even though we keep voting for it to be this way. I ran for office because western Pennsylvania is my home, too. Always will be. And I love it, and I hate it, and I want to leave, and I don't want to feel like I have to leave anymore. And I guess that's the confession I have to make. I ran for office partly to decide if I actually could stay here. Maybe more than partly. I am still not sure if I can. Losing did not help.

Yet I am a western Pennsylvanian. I feel that, deeply. Despite what it has wrought politically, I love my home region. Certainly I am most comfortable living in a small town than I am in a city even though cities offer an easier connection to others who share my politics. We have lived elsewhere, for that year in France and those few in Arizona. In some ways, France meant we lived in the apex of shared values. Public support for art. Actual respect from Parisians when they learned I was a writer (even though at the time the label was more conceptual than born of evidence). Good bread and cheese. Still, Paris could never feel like home. Its largeness felt as foreign as the language. Arizona, too, never stood a chance, despite its beauty and warmth. I am conditioned to love the lush landscapes of northern Appalachia and struggle with the flawed priorities of the United States.

Some days, that feels like a curse. Our futures are tied to forced abeyance. A fear that things could get even worse. That the threat of poverty, further decline, violent yahoos with

AR-15s, gay bashers, Bible thumpers, and petulant racists means we need to either get out or put our heads down and try to go unnoticed. We're trapped by how locality is defined, and by whom, and how being *not from here* is a relentless attack on the hope of our future. The real curse is Make America Great Again as the voicing of rage barely contained for decades.

Despite or because of all of this, I waver between love and hate. I ran for office on love, a troubled angry love, in the fashion of a dissatisfied partner willing to put in the work to save something that, in the right light, seems worth saving. I sometimes worry the relationship is irrevocably broken, and by that I mean the relationship between rural life and me, which remains at a crossroads. I also mean the relationship between rural America and American politics, which is marked by constant violent destructive abuse.

I want my home to open itself to generative forces. I want my home to be a place that recognizes the power of imagination and empathy. I want to be recognized as *from here* even when people vote to invalidate my claim. I want a different, better, fuller echo in the words on the sign by the giant flag beside the bridge. What I really want is to be able to say "Born here. Made here. Staying here" with hope and pride, not merely read it with despair and disgust.

THE POETICS OF POLITICS

On the eve of the 2020 election, in the tiny village of Springboro, Pennsylvania, the facade of the United Church glowed devilish red. Light cast down from a neon "Jesus Saves" sign over the front door. You might describe the effect as apocalyptic or sinister, and certainly you'd wonder at the design sense of red-glowing neon as a marker of Jesus. We have a fairly well-established palette of color metaphor, don't we? And throbbing red light on a darkened church generally suggests an inversion of the claim of this particular icon, about who you're for and who you're against. The church light's hue seemed like it was stumping for the other guy, the bad one, the creepy red-fleshed, fork-tongued, hoof-footed, promise-whisperer who exists in Western myth to remind us to be wary of the persistent siren song of evil.

I am writing about politics here, not religion. I am writing about 2020, and also 2016, and any number of times when the great collective *we* ignored the implications of figurative warnings. I am writing about rural America, and particularly rural Pennsylvania, and most specifically about the northwestern corner of my home state, where Appalachia and the Rust Belt converge and where the politics are described in single-word shorthand: aggrieved, resentful, angry, Trumpish.

In Springboro that night, I walked through the red haze to the back of the building, where I had planted a campaign sign carrying my own political logo. The church's social hall is the local polling station, where residents would arrive the next day to cast votes for either Donald Trump or Joe Biden, and also for either a fourteen-year, right-wing incumbent state representative or me, a mustachioed progressive Democrat running in a rural Pennsylvania district on a platform of universal healthcare, environmental conservation, and support for public education.

But I am also a college professor and writer, which naturally gets me to thinking about poetry and how the deepest fracturing of our national politics relates to a lack of poetic, narrative, and literary urgency. A poem is song and a dream and a lament and an elegy and a written document of the flourishing of human imagination. Politics is bereft, these days, of such impulses. Our intractable American political divisions exist because we ignore how the problems of politics are rooted in narrative, poetic, and lyric representations of our shared existence. All of this to say, when we're talking about politics and rural America we really, really, really need to be talking about metaphor, and story, and most of all, poetics.

* * *

1) "Let us suppose that everyone in the world wakes up today and tries to write a poem. It is impossible to know what will happen next but certainly we may be assured that the world will not be made worse."

2) The Commonwealth of Pennsylvania ought to stop offering higher ed grants to students who "major in poetry or some other pre-Walmart major."

3) "They made it sound like I was being critical of Walmart employees when I was really questioning taxpayers subsidizing college degrees that are unlikely to actually result in the graduate getting a job related to their degree."

4) "It seems to me that we cut ourselves off, that we impoverish ourselves, just here. I think that we are ruling out one source of power, one that is precisely what we need. Now, when it is hard to hold for a moment the giant clusters of event and meaning that every day appear, it is time to remember this other kind of knowledge and love, which has forever been a way of reaching complexes of emotion and relationship, the attitude that is like the attitude of science and the other arts today, but with significant and beautiful distinctness from there—the attitude that perhaps might equip our imaginations to deal with our lives—the attitude of poetry."

#1 is the poet Dean Young.

#4 is the poet Muriel Rukeyser, who used verse as part of her political activism. Her efforts included *The Book of the Dead*, a poem sequence that illuminates the cruel inhumanity of the industrial regime that caused an unknowable number of deaths among workers, likely measured in the thousands, who contracted excruciating lung-destroying silicosis during the construction of the Hawk's Nest Tunnel in West Virginia.

#2 and #3 are real utterances from Brad Roae, the incumbent I ran against in 2020. #2 is the reason I ran, quite specifically. He offered this idea in a 2016 memo to his GOP cronies in Harrisburg, outlining ideas on how to save money from the state budget by exerting old-fashioned anti-arts austerity. During our election cycle, he repeated the line several times, sometimes expanding it to "ancient Egyptian poetry" and often adding "women's studies" as an addendum. #3 is his 2016 response when the papers found out about his idiocy. In explaining himself, he clarified his preference for wage-busting, anti-union, big box stores over poets.

*   *   *

Politics is at heart a literary problem, because politics relies, like so much else, on a shared belief in stories. Yet the verses of politics offer repetitions of trope, cheap flatness, tired old stories of utility that cast each of us into stable boxes from which we are not permitted escape. And if you're from rural America? Well, then even stories intended to convey hope—Economic development! Job creation!—leave you mired in a definition of value that is labor and labor alone. Worse, your personal value, or even the value of a meaningful life, is defined only and always within the context of GDP. Thus the purpose of rural life is chained always to limited concepts of utility.

At any rate, if you are rural, you get to be dumb. Unsophisticated. Racist and bigoted and fearful and violent and all sorts of things that make up the persistent tropes of American rural caricature. Think about what you read about rural politics, about Trump Country and Red States and Flyover Country and the way my part of my home state is called Pennsyltucky and about how Democratic strategist James Carville defined Pennsylvania as Pittsburgh and Philadelphia with a lot of Alabama in between. *Democratic* strategist James Carville. Rural ridicule and abandonment remain some of the few remaining sites of bipartisan cooperation in contemporary America. It is the subject of every think piece about rural voters, most of which boil down to breathless claims that we rural folk are nothing but violent backwoods rednecks.

Well, I am rural. Born and raised on a farm in southwestern Pennsylvania, in a place still carrying surface residue from the coal industry that dodged out long ago in the 1970s. Slag piles dot our forests. You'll find abandoned deep mine portals, and gouged hillsides left behind from strip mining. And just as much as you'll see red-stained rocks in the creeks, you'll see red-stained political maps, where the virulent strain of contemporary "conservatism" overwhelmed the practical solidity of antique Eisenhower Republicans and replaced it with Donald Fucking

Trump. These are tangible signs—objective correlatives, even—of abandonment.

We haven't mattered for a very long time, and even when we have, we only mattered within the contexts of what our lives could provide for others. Bring back the coal mines, or reopen the steel mines, or frack the wells. We are only ever consumed, as per the design. The accepted social contract is that Appalachians live as embodiments of the resources exploited in their landscape. People and resources only matter as fuel for the prosperity of folks outside of the region. People and resources are burnt up and broken down, not by accident.

This is to say that I come from the "Alabama" portion of Pennsylvania, according to Carville, and his insult is a glaring example of the kind of condescension that drives so many Trump voters to gnash their teeth about "liberal elites." And it's also an example of how Democratic strategies are, themselves, glowing red neon signs declaring the intent to abandon both rural people and rural candidates who align with the Democratic Party. We are hardly anything more than castaways from a national political project, cannon fodder or collateral damage, or political sin-eaters who exist only to warn the civilized. We live as cautionary fables that make it easy for both the GOP and DNC to spitball easy vote tallies.

When you become a Democratic candidate in such a context, it's kind of hopeless, or feels like it is. But this is also the point of my running at all and for writing about losing. It is why I steadfastly believe that if there's any hope of breaking the partisan strangleholds of our nation, we need to examine the lyric and narrative sources of our losses instead of continuing to tsk tsk the rural rubes who "vote against their own interests" or offer self-congratulatory rhetorical gotchas about conservative hypocrisy and boring wonkish explanations of policy. We need to see that story is quite different from strategy and that politics is never, ever about policy and always, always about poems. And stories. And us. It's about all of us and how we learn to see each other through the consumption of literature spit out and consumed without deep consideration. We don't really read the literature of political America, not deeply, because as a nation we offer disdain for the practice of slow, careful, nerdy reading, which means we don't really read politics at all.

We live the stories we tell, and the stories told about us.

That's a line I used often during my campaign. I tried to frame my own political platform within the experience of being born and raised and still living in a part of the country that suffers. On the stump, I argued that much of our suffering relates to a long history of political storytelling, which means that as rural Americans we're cast always as the people who must suffer for the prosperity of the nation. Voting differently could be the writing of a new story.

In the reflective twilight of my (failed) election, within the context of the divided political landscape of our Trumpian America, I recognize that the larger pain of rural political failure is driven by a long legacy of hurt. I realize that the embarrassment and disappointment of losing to a mediocre politician is exactly the loss I have lived my entire life. Many of us live that life in rural America, where low-wattage leadership is fine as long as the person in that role can be fit through genealogy and ideology to the imagery that controls the rural political imagination.

This is an insult to the rural, to be clear. Because being rural means you are pilloried as inferior to the urbane, and local inferior leadership often rises to the top as a weirdo reinforcement of urbane tropes of the rural. In turn, rural politics becomes a new center of extractive ideology. As always, extraction means we, the rural, offer much and get nothing in return. That's the fate of rural Americans, ideologically and materially. We work so others can profit on our backs.

This is the history of both the Rust Belt and Appalachia, people valuable only because they can be put to work to generate wealth for others. A recalcitrant antipoetics signals disdain for the artistic capacities of humanity, let alone Pennsylvania college students. It reflects a desire to control the future of young people by politically determining the value of an education, and it is an abrogation of the capacity of hope in the lives of a region suffering the crushing heel of unrelenting industrial exploitation.

Do you see, then, why I couldn't not run for office when the dipshit in our state house seat called poetry useless?

* * *

Ben Lerner, in *The Hatred of Poetry*: "Thus hating poems can either be a way of negatively expressing poetry as an ideal—a way of expressing our desire to exercise such imaginative capacities, to reconstitute the social world—or it can be a defensive rage against the mere suggestion that another world, another measure of value, is possible."

* * *

Who gets to be a poet? That's the question I want to ask the incumbent, the fool who still gets to call himself my "representative," but it is a question I think we would all do well to consider in the context of the politics of rural America. The incumbent's indictment of poetic value buries the value of imagination under false terms of utility. He restates the claim that rural Americans are worthless unless they provide a specific kind of value to the economy, which is to say we're useless unless we render ourselves into the meat of industrial exploitation.

Poets, you see, are worthless, and so are rural Americans. This is the foundation beneath the claim to utility. We are poor so we have no choice but to submit to the big boxing attenuation of hope that marks the truest description of rural reality. We get dollar stores on every square mile, low wages that force us to shop there, and limited horizons to keep us stuck to both fates. Politically, it is self-defeating to point this out, of course, because winning elections relies on a weird optimism that things are fine even when they aren't, but also that things are about to explode if the other side gets or maintains or steals or expands power.

Yet poetry, as a concept, flourishes in the nuance of such contradictions, and it functions as an ordering of life in a way very different from politics. Poetry juxtaposes beauty and pain. In so doing, it destroys the false imagery of the collective Chambers of Commerce, which relies on the veneer of flourishing economies. Poetry, instead, imagines flourishing humanity, laments the absence thereof, and forces us all to live with the distress of how we often fall short of what we could be. The recognition of that shortness becomes the motivation for change, not just for a political reclamation, but a reckoning in how we get on living.

I am pro-poetry. That's why I ran for office, and how. Because the stakes of poetry are the stakes of humanity itself, and the reality of our days is bound by the refusal to take our lives seriously. The moment we speak of politics, we kick poetic impulse into the category of the luxurious. When we speak of politics, we consider poetry absent utility. We refuse to take seriously our desire for self-determination, for breadth and multiplicity and tolerance and choice and beauty. We, in effect, agree that poetry is a pre-Walmart major, and we believe this because we believe ourselves not worthy of poems. That's the message the nation delivers to us. In fact, the perverse message of Trumpism accurately recognizes the pain of not being taken seriously though it offers a cure that is only a rebooting of exploitation and degradation, built from the cinders of loathing.

* * *

Poetry again, also the disdain of it, how declarations against poetry are declarations against the hope of a different, better, flourishing future. There is no praise in MAGA, only destruction, which leaves no room for the light of hope.

A politician's antipathy toward poetry is a stand-in for the hatred of most exertions of the public good and a love song to the interests of money-mongering. Declarations against poetry echo as a marker of everything wrong with the philosophies of abandonment that shape our days in rural America. Austerity hates poetry, because poetry refuses the austere.

I have found life in the pursuit of the arts. My daily work is to share that value with others. I witness the everyday impact of stories, the ones that tether us to harmful histories and the better new ones, which we fashion ourselves, which break us free.

* * *

The poet Carmen Bugan: "Though the most urgent desire [of poetry] is self-liberation, the most ardent ambition is to find in language the tools with which to counteract injustice."

* * *

The stakes are high even in a small, backwater, state house race though it feels grandiose and self-congratulatory to say so. But isn't it here where Democracy will fail or persevere? Isn't it here where the right wing has taken root, overtaken and occupied the territory, and is now seeing the bloom of its strategy? Yes, it is here where violent authoritarianism threatens us all.

We live in a country balkanized by the ambitions of politics. The rural spaces of America, ignored by the loci of progressive power, have been occupied by autocratic, pseudoconservative militants, whose philosophies can be read as synonymous with white nationalism. This is not an exaggeration even if it is wrong to argue that every rural Republican is a white nationalist. They might as well be, though, because the political brand allows no nuance. Poetry, as a balm, revels in subtlety, works the fine distinctions of gesture and reality, gains force as it accumulates linguistic energy to fuel action. As Auden said, "poetry makes nothing happen." We need our nothings to become active.

If you didn't grow up in a place like here, and if you didn't read poetry about places like here, you may very well think there's nothing more to say about us. We are what we beget. It's easy to simultaneously rail against and ignore right-wing rural politics. When your own daily experience feels so distant from the headlines of yet another rural politician who wants to deny women bodily autonomy, outlaw the teaching of critical histories, or ban books, it's easy to simply move on. Fight where the fighting has a chance. As in, why worry about a Democratic strategy in places where Democrats have no history of success or even hope? As in, why support progressive campaigns in rural parts of the country when those candidates are just going to lose?

They are, right now. Lose, I mean. They surely will. But we need to consider the totalizing impact of ideological oppression, the power of antipoetics and petty grievance politics, and how these impulses have nearly unfettered power in rural Pennsylvania and, indeed, the country.

Think about why even nominally leftish policies are considered too radical for the mainstream Democratic Party, and think about how in some way rural voters are often the ones blamed for tepid Democrats. Campaign platforms have to appeal to "the heartland." Somehow that means we never get to hear candidates push for rural issues that matter. For example, universal, public-option healthcare would change lives in rural America, where many have no insurance or poor insurance and cannot leave bad jobs because they'd lose what little they get from their employers' plans. A green industrial revolution would preserve our natural spaces and offer new jobs. Such issues should be at the forefront of every rural campaign. Every one.

Of course they are not, because the mainstream Democratic Party refuses to support such public investments with full voice because they fear losing "moderate" voters, who live in places where such ideas appear radical because they are insulated from the very real consequences of generational abandonment. Suburban voters. Generally wealthy, white ones. These are the moderates who the DNC courts and represents, and who turned out for Donald Trump, because in the quiet of the ballot booth the siren song of lower taxes, itself a fantasy of spun lies, matters more than the reality of the suffering poor. In the end, rural Americans get to be the excuse for those votes and for the inaction of the "moderates" because we are the allegedly foolish voters who won't support the things we need. So none of us gets what we need, and rural Americans get to carry blame for the domination of the right wing.

I know. I know. It's not terribly insightful to argue that the divisions between rural and urban America lie at the core of the crisis of our twenty-first-century politics. But even that familiar observation fails to consider the way political stories trap us. It is not a stretch to argue that our political division relates to the way horizons are built, or rather how they are reinforced, by the stories we have come to accept and now expect.

Let's put it differently. How many Democrats think poetry should be central to the revitalization of economically devastated regions? How many Democrats are willing to fight for the arts as a top-line budget priority? Recently, I witnessed a crass turn by so-called moderate Democrats, who began lauding school book bans done transparently instead of maintaining the position that all school book bans, whether transparent or covert, are simply bad. Politicians are part of the shallow-reading cohort that thinks Robert Frost's "The Road Not Taken" is an inspiring lesson about finding your own way, instead of an indictment of the poseurs who take the easy way but tell the story of how much harder their chosen path happened to be. Toxic moderation is watching extremists ban LGBTQ+ books and taking the easy path of saying, "Let's just be sure we ban these books the right way." How many political Democrats can hold the line against extremist GOP agendas without ceding ground in the pursuit of mythical "moderate" angles?

Too few. Far too few. Thus we need art and we need poetry more than ever. Poetry, as a resistance, encourages expansiveness. Politics demands containment. Poetry finds meaning in the outsider, the sideways view, the ironic, the complicated, the disastrous, the beautiful, the decayed. Politics always asks which way the wind is blowing, and follows suit. Poetry creates value when the political won't allow it. Thus a politics that denies the value of poetry seeps from the mouths of both the stupid and the strategic because poetry is our way out of this. And so few who know how politics actually works want a way out. The system works, for them.

*   *   *

"I believe in the divinity of profligacy," Dean Young writes. "The creation of art, okay, just the attempt at the creation of art, as well as the appreciation of it, is both an enlarging of the world and an expanding of consciousness. To write a poem is to explore the unknown capacities of the mind and the heart; it is emotive, empathetic exercise and, like being struck by lightning, it will probably leave you stunned, singed, but also a bit brighter, and too your odds of being struck again then go much higher."

* * *

I ran for the Pennsylvania House of Representatives because I grew up in a place that hates poetry even though its daily existence is poetic dry kindling. I ran because I live, now, tucked away in the northwest corner of the state two hours from my hometown but exactly the same, because this region made me who I am—committed to art, music, literature, learning, justice, kindness, equity, peace, democracy—despite the best efforts of political narrow-mindedness and against the tropes others refuse to disbelieve.

* * *

I am tired of losing.

I don't want to lose anymore, or again.

I don't want us—a great expansive inclusive dreaming *us*—to be cast as the ones who must always lose.

A hard truth: We have the politicians we deserve. Donald Trump, for example, was no aberration. Trump is what we currently are, what we have allowed. It is what America is and America allows. He's the monstrous stupid creation that smashes our faces into the mirror. Hello, America, this is you. He should have provoked a moment of reckoning, across the political spectrum. *Oh shit*, we should say, *this is what we have become.* Instead, we turned him into a political demigod.

We lose when Republicans gin up fear and violence and hatred to get votes inside our borders. We lose when Democrats paint us as deplorable gun-clinging hillbillies, as suffering sorry backwater nobodies, who keep voting *against our own interests.* This is how we lose, over and over again, because we've been abandoned to loss.

Because we lack the capacity to imagine the complexity of a rural poetics, American rural life is plagued by right-wing infection. Caricatures open wallets for Republican and Democratic candidates both, because hard-edged political blocs are efficient for campaigning. Outrage is a great way to raise money and lock in votes. Rural Americans in turn become sacrificial oddities suffering in the wilderness. We live the same tired stories that have always been told about us. We're backward Appalachia, the industrially collapsed Rust Belt, the doomed.

But there don't have to be losers. I said that in my campaign, and I say that now. If we accept there must be, we will always, always, always be the losers. We need the space to imagine what sticking up for ourselves might mean. We need space for people who try to stay and fix things. We need to reject the idea that wanting better means we don't belong.

* * *

Jane Kleeb is not a poet but, instead, a Democratic organizer and chair of the Nebraska Democratic Party. In *Harvest the Vote*, she writes: "As Democrats, we simply have not offered another choice to rural voters. We have not shown up to listen to the issues they care about. We have not looked to rural people for ideas. We have not invested in rural candidates. We abandoned state parties, the backbone of all elections, in rural states."

* * *

I believe in the capacity of new stories as vehicles of meaningful change. Our shared disease is a congenital failure to read and understand the stories we are forced to live over and over. Democrats are *this*, and Republicans are *that*. Rural people care about X, and urban elites care about Y. We stay poor because this is a politics that works at the ballot box, because we lack the narrative literacy to imagine our way out of the fate delivered to us.

"God, Guns, Country," as some of the many disturbing Trump signs around here read during the election. There are pictures of AR-15s on those signs. Of course there are. An AR-15 is a poem, in the worst way I can imagine.

Politicians forget or perhaps never read or, even worse, know the precise risks of allowing the presence of Thomas Gray's "mute inglorious Miltons" to lie in anonymity in country graveyards. Politicians ignore or fear the reality of poets like Aafa Michael Weaver, who wrote verse in his head while driving a forklift around a warehouse. They don't know the verses of Steve Scafidi, who makes a living as a cabinet maker and makes his readers feel more alive through his rollicking poems. Politicians see and persistently defend the profits of industry as a just use of a life, denying what could be if we allowed for a different sense of value, measured in dreams. We are taught to accept a general cleaving of opportunity, that the zip code of our birth presumes our industrial fate. You are not allowed to be an artist if you are rural, and you cannot be rural if you are an artist.

As a nation, we refuse to learn those lessons. We refuse to see politicians for what they are: symbols of our fidelity to a poetics that consumes us and destroys us and calls it a triumph of the American dream. Who we vote for reveals our inner lives, how we have been wounded and by whom, and how we wish to rebuild or scorch the earth to settle that score. We are led to believe ourselves no better than what we already have. Or, maybe worse, we know how little we have, so we're not going to risk asking for more. Just don't make the abusers mad, and at least only a quarter of us will live in abject poverty.

Dark poetry, indeed.

But shouldn't we also ask ourselves to name our favorite rural poet? I mean, a really rural one, born and raised and still there. And when you think of the poet, do you think they speak for only themselves, or only for people who live where they do, or write as windows into places only they know? Or can rural poets sing to us all? This is a vital question because the poetry we assign value also reveals much about our shared hearts and commitments.

When we value only that which pushes us where those in power wish us to be, we suffer generational harm. We are told things cannot get better because better will not be permitted. Our grandest hope becomes paying the bills, maybe. In places like where I live, even that seems more and more a useless fantasy.

We need a fresh rural poetics, one that refuses to accept clunky old angry verses.

* * *

This is a book of dreams. I don't know if that's hope, but I'd like to think so. It's trying. The campaign was trying.

"There is no other way work of artistic worth can be done. And the occasional success, to the striver, is worth everything," Mary Oliver writes in *A Poetry Handbook*. "The most regretful people on earth are those who felt the call of creative work, who felt their own creative power restive and uprising, and gave to it neither power nor time."

Artists imagine the world into being. They gather the detritus of experience, then reassemble the parts into new forms. Those forms show us the world as it was, as it is, and as it can be. Such visions resist tyranny, which explains why totalitarians imprison artists and why calls to defund the arts are a pernicious undermining of democratic ideals. Poets are dangerous to autocrats. This is the real point. Whether they know it or not, politicians who devalue poetry do so because poetry threatens the bullshit narratives that keep them in office.

To defund poetry, then, is to demand the end of critique. It is a coward's vision of austerity as a means to demand a usefulness measured in the way rural bodies must be sacrificed to contribute to a narrow definition of economy. It is a call to legislatively control bodies, what they can do and what they are good for, because the politically small-minded fear an awakening.

I reference "bodies" literally, in the sense that the hard, "useful" work of our nation—miners in the tunnels, laborers in the factories and mills, nurses in the hospital wards, farmers on the land—takes a toll on the body. Bodily work wears out knees and backs, blackens lungs and shortens lives. If you didn't see this cruelty before, you saw it during Covid, when the laborers of our nation were the people forced to keep close-contact work without adequate protections to their bodies or their livelihoods. You should have seen it before, in every antiworker campaign to limit union membership, in calls to weaken OSHA, to roll back environmental standards, to punish and shame folks on public assistance, to meet protests against state violence with state violence. To make bodily autonomy itself illegal.

When politicians call poetry a "pre-Walmart" major, they are making it clear who gets to decide for themselves what they want to be. They make it clear who is allowed to dream and imagine, and who cannot. *Be useful* is a demand shouted at the impoverished. *Fuck poetry* is the clarion call of the small-minded. *Get to work* follows both, work defined in a way that benefits someone other than you.

Artists are dangerous because they inspire change. Art speaks back against the narrowing of horizons championed by political violence. There's little more politically dangerous than rural poets and artists who defy the narrative delivered as the way things are. Artists widen the lens of experience, and such expansiveness demands a vision that refuses to accept the limitations rural demographics imply.

Put another way: Politicians call art frivolous because they fear its power, and they rhetorically exile those unlike them because a reckoning of difference threatens the power the rural right clings to. If we embrace compassion, care, openness, tolerance, and equity as rural values, then the conservative stranglehold ends.

* * *

It started snowing the night before the election, right on cue. November in northwestern Pennsylvania, and it's all over. "The winds of change," I called it the day before in a quick cheeky online campaign post. Gusts blew my campaign signs back and forth. Snow would follow.

Shortly after leaving the red glare of the Springboro United Church, melancholy arrived. I remember it as a distinct moment, the flipping of a sudden switch. My car was filled with sadness. I knew it was over, not just the long campaign but the sense of possibility the campaign offered. I knew I would lose, in a more visceral way than ever before, even though I knew always, from the very first moment, that I would.

As I drove around the rural corners of the district planting more signs at polling stations, the snow gathered. I steered the back roads in quiet dark, making my stops. I waded through deepening flakes to place signs outside township builds and churches and volunteer fire halls.

It was over, all of it. I had no chance and never did. I questioned, not for the first or last time, whether it had been worthwhile.

Worthwhile is another important word here, about what counts and who counts and how predestination might be a theological concept likely preached about in the devil-red-neon-illuminated church, but also a deeply political reality for those of us who live in places like northwestern Pennsylvania, large swaths of rural America you probably don't often think about but, if you do, probably know as Flyover Country or Trump Country or simply as the red portions of election night maps you write off as losses even before elections begin.

Thus my losing is not really a shock or even uncommon. I was a Democrat, and even worse a *progressive* Democrat, someone the incumbent called "the most ultraliberal" challenger he'd ever faced, while his backers called me a socialist and a baby killer. They said my mustache made me look like Stalin or Trotsky. Again, no surprises there. Not even creative insults.

In the red-glowing church in Springboro, Pennsylvania, two-thirds of the voters of 2020 cast their ballots for Trump and for the incumbent and for the antipoem they know by heart. This is pretty much how it went across the whole county, and pretty much how it always does these days in rural America, where the best you can do as a Democrat is get some credit for showing up to get crushed at the polls.

I ran and I lost. There it is.

Candidates like me may be destined to lose in places like where I live. The outcome is inevitable, at the moment.

My earnest questions, then: How is our losing in this perpetual way helping us out? How is it helping you? Losing is kind of all we've got, right now. We need to find ways to lose better, until we start not losing. We need to understand that our rural losses are national ones, global ones, markers of creeping decline and the consequence of turning, always, the other way when suffering persists.

Politics as song? Politics as poetry? Politics as the art of living? Yes. Yes. Yes it can be, I think, or at least I want to imagine that possibility. Politics is a narrative problem, in the end. We need a poetry of rural hope, an artistry of anti-utility. We need to sing songs of our worth. We need pre-Walmart majors so we can live a post-Walmart life.

MIGRATIONS

We followed the lonely ribbon of US 40 through creosote bush desert broken only by occasional dusty side roads and sun-bleached roadside lean-tos. Emptiness flooded the landscape of New Mexico, dried waters stretching across the memory of alluvial plains. Faced with the unbroken flatness of the landscape, we bet on our eyesight. Spot a distant point on the horizon, mark the odometer figures, drive on while the miles wind upward. In that way, you can find the limits of your vision. Our best distance exceeded one hundred miles, the peak of a distant blue mountain that seemed to get no closer for hours. Eventually, I forgot to notice its glacial approach—and our game—until without warning we entered rolling foothills. Soon after, we climbed into the blessed cool of pine forests, passed through a small resort town, and then descended into another stretch of flatness.

It is the emptiness, in the desert, that defines location, at least for me. It is the empty spaces between brief towns that make the towns stand out. Even small clusters of homes carry significance, surrounded as they are by barren desert. In the populated East, one settlement flows into the next. In the desert, there are places and emptiness, neither fully itself without the proximity of the other.

Late that day, we stopped in Alamogordo, a small town skirting the White Sands Missile Range. There, we celebrated the official start of my father's retirement, the day the paperwork became final. A genial waiter offered a campy rendition of Frank Sinatra, slipping "retirement" into the lyrics of a crooning Happy Birthday song. That night, Independence Day fireworks exploded silently at the foot of a mountain outside of town. All of this happened in a world that no longer exists. The summer of 2001. Before 9/11. Before Covid. Before Trump.

The next morning, we pressed on into Arizona, where a rare thunderstorm met us at the border. The air flooded with the fresh scent of watered sage brush. But even in the mist, the unmitigated desert remained: bare rock mountains, low-scrub mesquite, ocotillo just starting their monsoon season bloom. We drove through this landscape, where settlements appeared only as signs directing us to leave I-10. The towns themselves barely dented the emptiness, usually hidden in valleys off the main corridors when they appeared at all. Just as with New Mexico, side roads offered the suggestion of new places while the main drag led on without pause.

* * *

I'm getting to a point here about migrations and flow and the legality of existence and the indignity of nativist claims and

the collapse of politics into what we know is a ridiculous racism-
driven discourse of "border issues." I am getting to the point of
what it means to be called an "illegal alien" by race-baiting,
right-leaning politicians who refuse to stop dehumanizing desperate people. I am getting to the point that I, too, have lived
that way, with obviously lower stakes. Much of this relates to
home, definitions of it, who gets to claim it, and how the structures of politics are just one of many ways to alienate human
beings from places where they might choose to make a life.

*　　*　　*

Jen and I came to the desert in the newness of our second year of
marriage. The move was motivated by banal academic reasons,
related to a Ph.D. program in Tucson I would quit after a single
semester. We set up our freshly partnered life in the town of
Sierra Vista, a high-desert place about an hour from the city. Jen
taught French at the local high school, and we bought a house.
From our backyard, we could see the peaks of the Huachuca
Mountains. In the climate of the desert, the peaks were the only
way to witness the seasonal shifting of green to blazing yellow
autumn aspens to snow caps.

Otherwise, the desert was the desert. Scrubby, without the
archetypal cactus you see in Western flicks and Snoopy cartoons.
Our landscape was filled with the muted olive and ochre of creosote bush, ocotillo, and mesquite. When I traveled the I-10 cor-
ridor to Tucson, the desert grew into taller saguaro forests. There
the desolation of the empty space between things seemed more
profound: the first road sign announcing the Tucson city limits

rests alone in the desert, followed immediately by a sign list-ing the city as twenty-three miles distant. In the winter, the first visible cue of the city appears as a brown bubble of haze hang-ing in the blue sky over Tucson, pollution trapped by the vagaries of temperature inversions.

In this wide space, illogical housing developments appear like oases or mirages. They are improbable outposts, patches of feudal-like engineering. They fortify themselves against the desert with concrete block walls, huddle together in tight out-croppings of identical homes that refuse the countless acres of empty land nearby. They seem like daring attempts to populate nowhere, but they strike me also as sad fortifications against emp-tiness. They shoulder together against cold nights, squirm to find the safest position. I wonder if they were born, these neigh-borhoods, or if they were exiled, cast into the desert to stare at the moon and ponder the languished cries of night air that must always be held at bay.

Residential outcroppings deny the presence of emptiness, exerting themselves as more than, or superior to, or even not part of the surrounding desert. They exist only at the expense of the spaces between, forcing the desert to submit to their walls. They are destinations that seek identity alone and, worse, refuse the potential of wandering night animals. They wish to be left alone, above all else. They wish to be safely cut off, where desert space vanishes behind tall walls, where the saguaro are replaced by irri-gated lawns.

I prefer the emptiness of possibility. Or, rather, prefer to think about the capacity for transit within all deserts, literal and figurative, quiet nighttime stirring and aching nighttime coyote howls, and the hope of wild things visiting disparate settlements as a way to remind us that walls, borders, differentiation have no claim, not really. Or shouldn't.

* * *

Whether natural or cliché or both, the impulse to move away is real. Maybe this is one of the markers of my Appalachian roots, or just the wanderlust of youth, or my own idiosyncratic desire to look yonder. Even now, as I approach fifty, I snag real estate booklets in every place I visit. I wonder, always, about the prospects there, wherever it is. I fall in love, frequently, with the imagined life of a new space.

Still, I always feel the draw back home, less as an urge to go back and more as a comfortable ease when I am there. The nature of the smoothed-off Pennsylvania mountains. The way a hayfield or pasture peaks through a wooded hillside. The curve of a creek headed into a valley. I haven't told you much about living in Arizona. I haven't even told you about living in Paris at all, and already I am home on the page. I am always home in my imagination or, rather, my imagination lives always in the landscapes of my birth. I see forests when I close my eyes, towering oaks and lush maples. I love even trash trees, like the staghorn sumac, that line highway cuts. I see roads curving echoes of the stream at the bottom of the hill. I see Pennsylvania as home.

Such affection was partly the effect of living in Arizona. I'd never had reason to dream of the trees of home until I left them. In the desert, I was at first so taken by the exposed geology and naked prickliness of the desert that I found myself writing about it. But almost immediately, the lushness of Pennsylvania forests emerged in my writing. Going away launched the ache for home. Being away confirmed the southwestern Pennsylvania mountains as the only place where I feel fully home or even fully myself.

Maybe leaving is a crucial step to feel love. Or maybe, at least, it is crucial for those of us who are made to feel like our homes are not really for us. This is the Appalachian rising in me again: We grow up in an atmosphere of decadence, seeing the daily residue of abandonment. The creek at the bottom of the family farm still swirls in rainbows from long defunct coal mines that wind beneath it. Rusting buildings indicate industry that ended. Great heaping bony piles appear in the forest, expanses of black too inhospitable to allow the forest to reclaim the space.

In Appalachia we grow up, also, understanding the way people not from where we are from see us. Rather, how they don't see us. They see the stories told about us, and the only thing more insulting than the stereotypes are the accuracies. Sometimes, the two are almost indistinguishable. Think about "deplorables" here, and think about how years after the 2020 election loss of a craven wannabe dictator, his middle-finger-flipping political signs still grace many front yards.

This is part of the going away. This is part of the exile of growing up in the red-stained places on the map. I mean that doubly, as an indication of the tainted color of many of our waterways and as the metonymy of our tainted politics. Our creeks are stained by the continual seeping of mine acid from mines that no longer employ anyone and, when they were open, enriched people who mostly never lived in our region. Our current politics are tainted by a false fidelity to The Big Lie and the conspiracies that gave rise to sneering but, sadly, accurate memes as the nation became mired in Trumpian ugliness: *But Her Emails* became a biting refrain of both the far right and the bemused ironic verse of the left. The image of one of those memes, a still shot of the father and son walking the postapocalyptic landscape of the film version of Cormac McCarthy's *The Road*, was filmed just up the road from where I now live. The natural beauty of Erie's Presque Isle State Park served as the ideal landscape for an imagined future America that had declined into chaos and violence.

But I love it. The place, I mean. Not the ideas. Often, not the people. I feel hatred and bitter resentment with unhealthy frequency, in fact. That will happen when you're from a place that seems to hate you, that has sent signals since you were a boy that you'd be better off heading away and forging a new life in a more hospitable environment like, say, the arid desert, or Paris, or anywhere you might be able to assume the person standing next to you in the grocery store might vote for, say, *you* and not the other guy. Or a place where, just spitballing here, you aren't told you are an unwelcome interloper to the region where you have lived almost your entire life. It's an odd position, really, being labeled as an outsider to the place where you were born, where you became you, and worst of all is the only place you have ever really loved and fear might be the only place you ever can love.

* * *

Sierra Vista is a mostly military place, dominated by the influence of Fort Huachuca. Most days, a border-monitoring blimp called "The Aerostat" floats above the city as a reminder of the politics of the nearby border, which are less about what it is like living there and more about the dark imagination of people who make a living stoking fears about invasions. It's twenty miles, give or take, to Mexico. The mountain range I used to watch beyond our backyard is the dividing line.

After quitting my Ph.D. program, I started traveling frequently toward those mountains, then hanging a left into the open grassland of what is called the Miracle Valley. There, the San Pedro River cuts across the middle of the dry plains. From a distance, the San Pedro suggests itself as a nightly flow, marked by towering cottonwood trees edging the north-flowing river. In gentle summer winds, dry grasses wave on the western side of the river, flatland hemmed in by the San Pedro and the craggy Huachucas. On the eastern side, the land climbs out of the river into rolling scrub, and here the spindles of creosote bush, ocotillo, and mesquite take over. Along the river, there are trees and greenness, relief from the ochre and olive that dominate elsewhere.

As far as rivers go, the San Pedro hardly seems to deserve the name of *river*. In most spots, it looks like little more than a ditch, a flattish, slow-moving trickle that carries less water than the tiny unnamed stream in the backyard of my parents' Pennsylvania home. Yet the San Pedro must be considered mighty. It remains one of the last free-flowing rivers in Arizona. This alone is praiseworthy. Other, grander waterways have been dammed, hemmed, and redirected to hydrate cotton fields north of Tucson or to provide drinking water for the millions who have come to call Phoenix home. No one has bothered to tinker with the San Pedro, perhaps because of its relative insignificance. In that, the river lives on, offering what it can to the parched landscape between Sierra Vista and Bisbee, a riparian zone of lush grass, turtles, snakes, frogs, and trees, a yearlong flow of water in a region that typically follows a drought-flood cycle. Above all else, the San Pedro is steady.

Water, of course, defines the desert. Or, rather, lack of water. The great distinction of Arizona's Sonoran Desert is its relative abundance of rain compared to other deserts, twelve inches a year that create a thorny desert tapestry of saguaro cactus, barrel cactus, cholla, ocotillo, creosote bush, palo verde, yucca, agave, and mesquite. The saguaro, notably, drops away in the higher, cooler Chihuahuan Desert that most closely resembles the land around where we lived. Scant rainfall nevertheless creates lushness in the Sonoran Desert, a spring bloom of immense beauty and a year-round cover of vegetation that stands in contrast to the clinically arid and empty Mojave Desert of California and Nevada. There, only the Joshua tree seems to suggest life. The rest of the land stretches on flat, dry, crusted.

I often crossed the San Pedro on Highway 92, headed to the tiny border town of Naco, which has a much larger Mexican twin immediately over the rusted steel fence that marks the US border—a border that, for many, separates the US, that is, *us*, from *them*. I came here to play golf, the beginning of a period of my life that combined questionable success as a freelance writer with unquestioned failure as a professional golfer. My career earnings as a freelancer were about $500; as a golfer, I only lost money to travel and tournament fees.

The now-closed Turquoise Valley Golf Course and RV Park sits nearly adjacent to the border in Naco. It laid claim to a history as the longest continuously operating course in the state of Arizona unit it was sold, sold again, and then shuttered. Same story, different place: Rural losses are a commonality that supersede regional differences. The original club opened in 1908 in nearby Warren, then relocated to Naco when the WPA built a nine-hole course in 1936. In the winter, the RV park used to fill with Canadian snowbirds, making Naco a tight combination of the three nations of North America.

Here, the gorge of Greenbush Draw ushers water from Bisbee, and from the golf course, toward the San Pedro. Much of the year, the draw runs dry, or barely runs at all. During the summer desert monsoon, it often gurgles as heavy waves of chocolate water sling toward the river. On mornings after heavy rains, muddy streaks five feet wide cut across the golf course, residue from the water that rushed from Mexico into the draw, from there to the San Pedro and on north.

On US maps, Naco barely registers, other than as twin flags marking it as a border crossing. As a place, Naco languishes in the shadow of its hipper, bigger next-door neighbor, Bisbee. Five miles away, the gaping pit of Bisbee's Queen Mine proves the bigger town's worth. Once the grandest of the old copper towns, it claimed to be the biggest city between St. Louis and San Francisco. Now, Naco plays the ugly little sister to Bisbee, which boasts artful renovations of classic Western hillside homes. Naco hides dented trailers next to adobe military barracks riddled long ago by Pancho Villa's bullets.

But from the base of the Mule Mountains, which save downtown Bisbee from the sight of the border, Naco's size becomes apparent. The Mules flatten out toward Naco, lengthening to a plain that runs into Mexico before gradually rising to a small outcropping of spiky mountains south of the border. Viewed from the mountains, Naco shows the imbalance of its twinness. Hundreds live in Naco, Arizona, thousands in Naco, Sonora. A thin ribbon of ten-foot wall separates the two, the barrier extending perhaps a mile from end to end before giving way to open desert. Naco, counted as a single town, rivals Bisbee in size.

It is Naco, not Bisbee, where the US Border Patrol keeps an office and where US Customs mans an official border crossing. And it is here where thousands of unofficial border crossings start. At night, Border Patrol agents and migrants play a high-stakes game, pitting low-tech runners against high-tech thermal cameras.

When I drove to the golf course in early mornings, I often passed Border Patrol trucks, some scoping the highway, some driving back to headquarters after a long night. I often passed trucks parked on the side of the road, agents working the desert on foot. Sometimes I saw the surveillance vans, the ones with telescoping radar units jutting twenty feet into the air. Sometimes I saw the buses, surrounded by groups of twenty, thirty, even forty captives sitting on the ground. Men, women, and children, most of them wearing heavy flannel shirts and blue jeans, working clothes. The buses would soon take them back to Mexico, where they would face the same impossible struggles that inspired their desperate attempt to reach a better life in the United States.

The Border Patrol isn't alone in monitoring the desert. In remote spots, tall blue flags mark water stations set up by humanitarian groups. It's hard crossing the desert, and far too many migrants die of thirst after being abandoned by conniving coyotes. Tighter restrictions near border towns push the migrants into more and more remote locations, where the risk of capture is lower but the risk of death much higher. Humanitarian groups—rabble rousers like Catholic nuns and middle school math teachers—recognize the way border politics plays out badly for human beings trapped by the rhetoric of violence, so they set up water stations. At the same time, self-styled patriots arm themselves with night vision goggles and tactical rifles, find the water tanks and wreck them. They dump the water into the dry earth, thinking of themselves as heroes in some existential fight for God-knows-what.

Imagine that pain for a moment, migrants with dry-cotton mouths, worried about how they will make it much farther. Their lips are cracked, their tongues a wooden lump. This wasn't what they signed up for, not what they had been sold. They forked over a wad of cash for safe passage, only to find themselves wandering in an empty desert without a map and a now-empty plastic milk jug fashioned as a canteen. They see the tank, and they feel the relief, salvation. They arrive, and it is full of holes, or knocked over, or befouled, all of this a signal of hatred and cruelty because wrecking a humanitarian water buffalo does nothing to stop a border crossing. It only harms those whose daily desperation has led them to believe in the mythical reputation of the United States as a place of refuge and reinvention.

When we lived in Arizona, vigilante groups were just starting to get national press. They rigged their own unmanned drones out of model airplanes and digital cameras. Now, they'd just buy cheap toy drones from Amazon. The vigilantes posted footage of crossings and border agent apprehensions on their website, using the images to fan conspiracies about "invasions." They went out on their own nightly armed patrols, too, searching for and capturing migrants themselves. They posted these pictures on their websites: ghostly night-vision photos of people moving through the desert, pictures of an overweight middle-aged white woman guarding the migrants she caught herself. These photos have a grating familiarity. They look almost exactly like the photos that run in my hometown newspaper after the first day of deer season, beaming hunters holding the blood-smeared head of the deer they bagged.

* * *

We left the desert after three years, relocating to Paris while Jen finished a graduate degree in French culture and language. I spent my days roaming the city, with a particular affection for the American Library of Paris. I wrote some, fiddling with a manuscript that would never see the light of day, and I played golf. I crossed the borders to Germany and Spain to compete in tournaments on what was then called the European Professional

Development Tour. Jen and I lived in a tiny apartment, and ate tremendous cheese, and I learned enough French to retrieve our daily baguette at the *boulangerie* without her assistance.

I think it matters, however, that I always felt out of place in France. I think it matters that I felt lonely and often afraid. I speak enough French to get by, but not enough to understand the bulk of a conversation or, crucially, be seen as anything other than an American. I think the day of our arrival matters, too, when we rode from the airport to our new apartment, when I watched artless tenements pass by outside the van window, cheap construction not shown on the postcards of Paris. I remember seeing Peugeots and Renaults, smaller, rounder, and at the same time more angular than American cars. I remember seeing motorcycles driven along the centerline, fast, to bypass slow traffic. All of it made me lonely, homesick.

We passed a narrow park somewhere in the city, where a homeless man slept on a dingy mattress. A hundred yards further, we passed a young woman in a swank tracksuit, holding a yoga pose. We drove through dim urban caverns, tall buildings blocking the sun. We broke free, just for a moment, passing a building I would later know as the Ecole Militaire, the site of Napoleon's tomb. Its gold dome gleamed, and I watched in wonder until we rounded a bend, back into narrow streets swathed in shadow.

Maybe an hour later, I stood alone in the gardens surrounding our new apartment building, waiting with the luggage while my wife fetched our French landlady. In time, I would accept the garden, even sit there on a bench and read in the sun. I would appreciate the way surrounding buildings formed a hollow space in the city, within which the sounds of rushing cars receded to white noise. That morning, though, waiting with our luggage, I looked above the grass and trees. I studied the vertical creases in the cement of our building and noticed where rainwater had made rusty streaks. I looked at the chipped corners of the balconies, where the cement had broken away to reveal rebar tips.

I waited there, alone in this French park, worrying that someone would stop, say hello. I wouldn't have known what to say, nor even understood whether they were greeting me or threatening me. I looked at my watch, still set to Pennsylvania time, hoping my wife would return soon. Around me, the air felt charged, not with the electricity of *l'amour*, but with something nameless and sinister. Even the sounds of traffic seemed different, muffled in an unfamiliar way, car engines exhausting a heavy French accent. I felt claustrophobic, not so much the walls of the buildings closing around me but the air itself. I felt the tightness and fear coming from within, an internal panic as my thoughts turned against me and hemmed me in.

Later, on the street, I smelled the city, a blend of bread dough, rubber, and rotting garbage. I saw the drift piles of leaves and dirt against the sides of the buildings, and a wide puddle left on a wall by a passing dog. I watched French men and women hurry by, some with baguettes, some pulling two-wheeled grocery trolleys. I stayed close to Jen, helpless and dependent. She found a phone booth on the street and called to set up our own apartment phone line. I crammed into the glass box with her, despite the rising temperature and stuffy confines, so I wouldn't have to stand alone, exposed.

* * *

In April of 2005, two years after we left the desert, one of the Arizona vigilante groups held a "revival" at the Miracle Valley Bible College, which lies fifteen miles west of Naco and three miles north of the Mexico border. At its entrance, a weathered sign advertises Friday fish dinners. The college itself looks as weathered as the sign, the white paint having long ago peeled to gray. Here, a thousand "Minutemen" convened, some paying a few dollars a day to sleep in the dormitories, others paying to park their RVs in the lot outside.

Nearby, the San Pedro trickled through its line of cottonwood trees. On both banks, dry grasses and baked red dirt slope toward the water, which itself slips under the border fence and runs north from Mexico. At its deepest, the San Pedro reaches an ankle. To call it a river seems generous. Still, the water allows the cottonwoods to thrive in a high desert otherwise filled with scrubby creosote bushes, low mesquite, and spindly ocotillo. Near the river, someone had parked a bright red bus. "Jesus Saves," white letters proclaimed, "Get Aboard the Salvation Bus."

Cochise County officials saw the Minuteman gathering less as a religious revival and more as a base camp, fining the college for neglecting to obtain the proper permits. On his website, the owner of the college claimed this as evidence of the devil's work to silence his message. He claimed the same thing about the time he wrecked his dump truck.

At least the Minutemen didn't shoot anyone. They descended on the Miracle Valley, took their lawn chairs to the border, sat for three weeks, and then went home. A raging success, they considered the event, confident their presence deterred hordes. To their minds, three weeks of armed presence stemmed the tide of a half million successful crossings a year. FOX News and CNN came down for a look. Newspapers sent reporters. Sometimes, reports mentioned the hundreds who die each year trying to make it across the desert. Sometimes, they did not, focusing instead on the newsworthy gathering of American citizens, the self-appointed militia and news media both content to ignore or forget the reasons why the border is crossed.

* * *

For me, becoming "illegal" started at the *Prefecture de Police* in Paris, where Jen and I delivered the documents necessary to begin the process of acquiring my official long-stay visa. Jen had a student visa and a bona fide reason for being in the country. I had neither. I was just the trailing partner with my vague titles of "freelance writer" and "professional golfer." We wanted to follow the rules, so we started the long official process.

If you haven't experienced French bureaucracy, however, you would be as unprepared as we were for an unknown capacity to screw up the rules by following the rules precisely. We'd been told that our first visit to the *Prefecture de Police* would be frustrating and result in an inevitable return visit. The office worker always says you have the wrong paperwork, we were warned. Indeed, that happened, after the long wait in a line of fellow migrants trying to follow the official process. Our secret weapon was Jen, though, whose French carries the kind of fluency that allows her to be unrecognized as American and, more importantly, deliver appropriate flaring Gallic anger when confronting inevitable bureaucracy.

The details of our saga are unimportant. They related primarily to definitions of "official" when applied to birth certificates, which essentially boiled down to the French *fonctionnaire* refusing to recognize any birth certificate not from France as legitimate. It's easy to laugh at that now, or even sniff at the utter French snobbery, except we faced almost identical roadblocks when we returned to the United States and the Pennsylvania DMV worker initially refused to recognize our Arizona licenses as equivalent to Pennsylvania ones.

Bureaucracy is a cultural obstacle that seems designed to alienate foreigners. In Pennsylvania, we combatted this alienation by being Pennsylvanian and refusing to be intimated. In France, Jen flared her nostrils and sighed in a way the French hear as, *oh shit things are getting real now*. The French *fonctionnaire* recognized game versus game and respected the strength of this American woman who wasn't going to take her *merde*, and that is exactly how I got my temporary visa stamped as approved, and my official appointment for the required medical examination.

Three months later, I rode the metro by myself to a distant *arrondissement* at the edge of Paris. Jen had class, and I had picked up enough French on the golf course where I spent my days to solo-navigate the next stage of the process. The appointment was primarily for a chest X-ray to make sure I didn't have tuberculosis, and that I wasn't going to infect France. We should just ignore the logic of that official appointment taking place three months after I'd arrived in France. Or, we should recognize that official immigration policy is as nonsensical in France as it is in the United States, where the system seems designed as a series of obstacles to block outsiders instead of as a rational process concerned with health and safety.

It was gray on the day I headed to my appointment, early winter arriving with typical wet Parisian cold. I wore a wool coat, I'd purchased in Paris, with the hope of blending in. I also wore nice slacks—Parisian trousers—instead of jeans. We'd lived in the city for months now, and I had studied the overall look of normal French people. I didn't have the style or money to present myself as refined, but I knew enough to look essentially local. At least I looked local enough that tourists frequently stopped me on the street to ask directions in halting French. They were relieved when I spoke English, and so well for a Frenchman! Real French people generally ignored me, as I intended.

At the official medical appointment, I joined the other immigrants in an overfull waiting room. Eventually, my number was called, and I entered the examination room where a French doctor mumbled something to me in French. I did not hear him, so I whipped out my practiced French *politesse* and offered my extensive vocabulary.

"Pardon," I said.

I remember his eyes, the utter disgust and annoyance as he locked my gaze. He sneered. He shouted the same phrase again, dripping with acid. In French, of course. Bitter, angry, fed-up-with-these-foreigners French.

All he was telling me was where to hang my black wool jacket, there on the hook. But what he was really telling me was he didn't have time for this, or for me, that I was a low and ugly stain on his day, dirty and perhaps subhuman. You have to believe me. He was as clear as the night air in Arizona.

I passed my medical exam and was given directions to return to *Prefecture de Police* for the next interview. That was that. But it wasn't, not for me. I refused to be treated this way. We had been following all the rules, doing what we were supposed to do, and all we got was bureaucratic irritation and withering anger. Enough was enough, I decided. That day, I became what conservative American politicians call, using dehumanizing language to persist in their demonization of fellow human beings, an "illegal alien."

I did not go to the next appointment. My visa expired. I continued traveling out of France to play in golf tournaments, which is to say I worked essentially under the table as an illegal worker. Except, since I was likely the worst professional golfer in Europe, I failed to actually earn any money.

In France, following the rules just became too much of a pain in the ass to continue. Enduring the process became too much a practice of demoralization. Plus what were the odds, really, that the *gendarme* would stop me on the street outside our Paris apartment, hear my American accent, and demand I produce documents proving I belonged? I could move invisibly in the city.

If you haven't experienced the dehumanization of immigration policy, in even a minor way such as my privileged self, you have no business denigrating people who wind up living in undocumented status. France has no more or less bureaucracy than the United States, and when you are from a different place, such processes are so alien they might as well be literally from another planet. The sneering doctor in Paris is the sneering DMV attendant in Pennsylvania is the sneering state representative fanning racist fears of "illegal aliens" stealing jobs is the same as all of the sneering politicians who know a good wedge issue when they see it. Angry people roam our deserts, intent only on punishing those whose lives don't fit their narrow visions of humanity, and they call themselves patriots. What they champion, however, is better described as the curtailing of hope, the defense of violent separation, and the reduction of humanity. Nothing is made great. Just ugly and crude and hurtful.

* * *

Sometimes, just driving down a back road in the empty Arizona desert, you'll find the way blocked by the Border Patrol. All drivers must stop and declare their citizenship to agents dressed in green, black guns on their belts. On the only highway running north out of Sierra Vista, they've even built a permanent turnout. I always hated stopping. I always resented having to pull off the road on my way to Tucson, resented having to proclaim my citizenship and prove my guiltlessness.

"How's it going," they said as I pulled to a halt. I watched them watch me from behind mirrored sunglasses. Often, one of the agents wore a straw cowboy hat.

"All US citizens on board?"

"Yes," I said, watching in my rearview mirror as a German Shepherd sniffed the side of my car. An agent led her slowly around the back, pausing at the trunk. I always worried she'd sniff something even though all I carried was a spare tire and a jack. The dog moved on, down the other side of the car.

I live here, I thought. I haven't been to Mexico in ages. I'm just headed out to dinner in the city with my wife.

"Yes," I told them. "All US citizens."

I didn't want to stop. I didn't think I should have to stop. I lived in a free nation, a place where I didn't expect border agents to stop innocent civilians on their way to dinner. What right did they have? What reasonable suspicion forces me to wait silently while a dog sniffs my car for contraband? But expectations mean little, here, where politics demand tight restrictions, where many see the intrusion of checkpoints and sniffer dogs as the price of freedom. It comes with the territory, such people might say. If you live at the border, you should expect such things.

I used to laugh at the boldness of the smugglers: fake FedEx trucks, counterfeit Border Patrol vehicles, a man disguised as a van seat, crouching in a hollowed-out cushion until a border agent saw the telltale sneakers. In the newspaper, these moments seemed innocent, like an elaborate game of hide and seek. The game seems less innocent up close, when the flatness of grainy photos gives way to the trembling reality of actual encounter.

The checkpoints reminded me of the drama of the border, of men and women stuck in daily fights for jobs, or for life. Waiting at checkpoints offered a reminder that I did not welcome, mostly because they forced me to think about serious things:

how much worse a checkpoint would be if I had someone hidden in my trunk, if I had brown skin, if I were huddled in the trunk. I didn't like thinking about the way my life intersected with the lives of those who met border agents with more dire consequence. I felt uneasy about the moments when this "game" intersected with mine, or about the way border agents and vigilantes, both, probably saw me as part of their team. Worst of all, I worried that I was. Whether I wanted to be or not.

I just lived there, doing my daily things. I went to the grocery store, even to Basha's Mercado where I could buy the best salsa tomatoes. I played golf. Down there in Naco. On the border. In the back corner of the Turquoise Valley Golf Course.

* * *

On the border, in the back corner of the Turquoise Valley Golf Course, I aimed toward the crumbling ruins of General Blackjack Pershing's adobe barracks and cut the corner. Ninety years earlier, Pershing led the troops who lived in the barracks, sent to defend this Arizona border and, more importantly, to catch Pancho Villa, the Mexican revolutionary who threatened to reclaim these lands that once belonged to his country. He dared the Americans to find him. They never did. Everywhere and nowhere, Blackjack said of Pancho, before eventually abandoning the old barracks, which now collect graffiti in Spanish and English. Not long before this particular round of golf, someone abandoned a dirt-red Volvo there, too, propped on cinder blocks. A starburst of glass glistened in the dirt, smashed out from the windshield.

Mexico lay just to my right, and had I aimed there instead I could have driven my ball over the border. Behind the tee, a white and green Border Patrol truck floated over the rim of desert chaparral, trolling the back road toward the main highway. A barbed wire fence runs the length of the hole, 230 yards, dividing the grassy course and the mesquite thickets around Greenbush Draw. I took a quick look at the turquoise flag planted in the lower half of the green, then settled in for the shot, waggled.

Maybe I thought again about the out-of-bounds hook that could ruin my day. Maybe that's why I glanced toward the empty draw. Or maybe a quick flash of movement caught my eye and interrupted my pre-shot routine. I don't remember. Maybe I felt the prick of eyeballs studying me, a wary survey that broke my concentration.

Crouched beside the fence, huddled close to the overhanging mesquite and rusty metal fence, two men stared at me. Both wore green and brown plaid shirts. Their chests heaved. Their faces shone in the relentless Arizona sunlight, glistening with sweat on what counted as a mild day. They wore long sleeves and trousers, but I could still see the tension in their limbs. Their legs were poised, not athletic but ready. One of the men raised up a few inches, then hunkered back into his crouch, hidden from every angle but mine.

This took no time, no click of a watch hand or change of a shadow. Our exchange was instantaneous and, at first, unconsidered. I saw the man look at me, and I looked at him. I hadn't yet thought the things that I later would. I didn't remember, as our eyes met, the slow-moving Border Patrol truck. I didn't think about the trucks I'd watched on other days, parked on the side of the road. I didn't think about the helicopter I'd once seen working this very draw, diving and swooping toward the desert, herding people like so many cattle.

I saw the white of the closer man's eyes as they locked on my own. From twenty yards away, a man's eyes are visible enough to read. This man, crouched and anxious, could read, or misread my own. I don't know how he saw my golf club, whether he thought himself unlucky to face an armed man so soon after making the crossing. I don't know how he saw me.

But his eyes bulged, wary. He knew about the white and green truck, even if I hadn't thought about it. In our frozen moment, he weighed his options: crouch where he knew he'd been spotted, or take his chances running, where he knew a uniformed border agent would likely catch him.

I thought about my water bottle. I remember it as a movie flash, a slow-mo shot of me tossing the men a half liter of tepid water. That movie was never made, forever delayed as I weighed my options. I also wondered if I should wait for the men to leave, or just swing away and launch my shot over them. I mean, I had a good game going. I worried I'd accidentally hook my shot into their bodies if I didn't wait.

"How's it going?" I said, with a wave.

The words had barely escaped my lips and the two men were gone. A quick contraction of muscle, a burst from squat to action, and there was nothing left to see but vibrating wire.

By the time I reached the green, a line of a half dozen marched in single file flowed by a uniformed Border Patrol agent. They'd been waiting, down in the draw. I remembered, then, the white and green Border Patrol truck driving down Quetel Road. I remembered saying hello, flushing the two men into the draw. I realized I'd helped, that my wave and greeting had exposed them to the waiting agents. There is nowhere outside of the politics of the border.

* * *

I imagine myself at the southern border. I imagine the daring required to risk not just the desert, not just the US Government's attempts to keep me out, but also the overbaked desire of a thousand armed citizens. The sun's hot here, direct and overhead, always ready to fry nerves and spur violence. The OK Corral is only twenty minutes away, a sign of the consequences of rash conflict.

I imagine hiding out in an abandoned ranch house, waiting for darkness. I slip through the wire fence that marks the border, feeling the scratch of a rusty barb. I hide in the brush, watching an elderly woman and a tough-looking man sit in lawn chairs, sipping coffee and chatting under the stars. I imagine not seeing them, not seeing the border agents, not seeing the helicopters, just knowing somebody in the desert waits to find me, catch me, and send me back, while someone at home waits for the dollars I hope to earn.

I imagine crawling through a culvert near Naco, a high moon casting too much light. I slip past the RVs parked at the

Turquoise Valley Golf Course, hundred thousand dollar rigs filled with sleeping Canadian snowbirds who crossed their own border with nothing more than the currency of their skin. I consider the sinister shape of Blackjack Pershing's barracks, the menace of a smashed-up, abandoned Volvo. I imagine sprinting from the dusty street to the grassy fairway of the golf course, running as fast as I can toward the thickets of Greenbush Draw. I imagine myself with the men who did the same thing during the day, in the afternoon, high sun, sweat trickling down our backs. We squat and watch a golfer kneel down to slide a golf tee into the ground, waggle, set. We hope he won't look, please don't look. But he does, and we are eye to eye. I want to melt into the American landscape, right there in the open field.

It is hard to be far from home. It is hard to be foreign. It is hard even when no one cares you're there, and no one will try to herd you into a bus, and no one will call you illegal, and no one will point to you as a symbol of everything wrong in their country.

I try to remember this feeling of fear, just as I try to remember the feeling of complicity I felt at Turquoise Valley and the guilt that I just kept playing golf. I try to remember what it feels like to be shouted at by a representative of the official process. I try to remember what it feels like to be human so I can try to remain human.

I think, also, about the border near me now. Toronto is a three-and-a-half-hour drive. Canada itself is only fifty miles, due north, in the middle of Lake Erie. No one cares about that border, politically. You see plenty of Ontario plates hustling down the interstate to shop at the outlet mall in Grove City. There are no Border Patrol checkpoints even though, technically, the law would allow them to be established and compel all of us to pull over and be searched. I imagine the outrage if that happened, from the very same people who are sure there is an invasion on the Mexican Border and who have told me, quite directly, that their perceptions have absolutely nothing to do with the color of skin that prevails on the people who make these different migrations. Legal is legal, they say. They believe themselves, I imagine.

*   *   *

Fridays on the golf course, late in the afternoon, I often heard amplified Spanish rattling through the air. Fast words, furious, imploring and foreign, echoed over the border fence, somehow angry to my ear. A rally, I first thought, something political and organized, some gathering of the citizens for a mad rush at the border. Pancho's back, ready for another crack.

Most likely, it was only the sounds of an open-air market, the words really just invitations to buy tomatoes cheap, to check out the fresh tortillas. But I like to think it was something else, the mustering of a resistance, a rally of those we call illegal, as if their very lives lack official validation. I like to think it was a Mexican inversion of the Minuteman Project, thousands gathering in a Sonoran Miracle Valley to declare humanity.

We're here, the words from the open-air market could be, and *we're not giving up. Go ahead and line up that shot, but listen to this. We're here, and we're not going away. This is how we talk, how we look, who we are. Go ahead, fence us in, go ahead, chase us out, go ahead, try.* Like words over a wall, like a river under a fence, we will flow.

FIVE

THE POLITICAL GRAMMAR OF THE COUNTY FAIR

At first, the region's goat farmers were amused by our squat, knee-high Pygmies, these tightly paunched animals so different from the high-hipped, loose-skinned Saanens, the cropped-ear LaManchas, and the classic-faced Alpines. With no category of their own, the Pygmies were forced to compete at the county fair directly against the larger dairy animals and presented no obstacle to their lanky struts.

My mother had taught us how to prepare, a woman who went from prim Catholic boarding school to formal Catholic women's college, whose high school rebellion amounted to the secret removal of required white gloves when visiting town. When she started a 4-H chapter that met each month in our family room, her first act was to teach farmers' children Robert's Rules of Order. She inked the words "I move" on a large rectangle of white posterboard and had my sister add a cartoon buck caught in the moment of attack, head down, curled horns pressing against the edge of the I. His instinctual act of fury signaled grammatical restraint; it was intended to stop us from using "motion" as a verb and, in turn, contain sloppiness of voice. We were to move that the minutes of the previous meeting be accepted, to move that we lead our goats along the town's main street at the local university homecoming parade. Our motion was toward refinement and clarity, learning to lead ourselves neatly in manner and language.

We learned to groom the goats as well. My mother showed us how to trim stray hairs from their udders, how to gently pull the bright links of plastic chain collars to force goat heads up, straightening their spines, how to reach an arm under goat ribs, lift, settle the animal's legs into a perfect rectangle. My sister practiced this art on her does, proven mothers to annual birthings of triplets and quads, palm-sized kids who spent part of each late winter in our mud porch sleeping in a towel-filled cardboard box between hand feedings. My own attention turned to a young wether, his castration preventing a future of adult buckhood and guaranteeing a tender disposition. I learned how to lead him in a circle though he rarely offered more than a sideways glance in resistance, rebellion having been cut away too.

* * *

If you have not been to a county fair, really been to a county fair, like slept overnight in the goat barn because people have been caught paint-bombing the sheep to sabotage the competition, you probably can't really understand a deep truth of the sort of visceral politics that unspooled into the raging 2020s.

If you have not wandered the merchandise stalls at the county fair, and marveled at the geographic oddity of cheap plastic cowboy hats fronted with neon blue faux feathers, and the Pennsylvania girls buying and wearing such hats, and the Pennsylvania boys buying and wearing the black t-shirts emblazoned with variations of skeletal deer heads or antagonistic gun-themed slogans or all manner of Confederate battle flags in, again, Pennsylvania, and the plush wolf head-and-galaxy-backdrop throw blankets you can buy to keep yourself warm on a chilly autumn night or that you use to huddle under at a campfire or which you and your beaux/beau might drape over your laps as you take a slow ride on the Ferris wheel for, 100 percent, only the purpose of staying warm and not, I repeat *not*, with any relation to the pull of teenage bodily gravity competing headlong with the strictures of Sunday morning lessons and the comforting opacity of polyester fabric, you probably cannot understand either the odd popularity of quasi-fascist political merch or why liberal gotchas of conservative *hypocrisy!* do not really have meaningful impact.

And if you have not simultaneously stood in line among all of this waiting to get your funnel cake or your apple dumpling, each hoisted out of one of the many carny trailers that spend summers caravanning from fair to fair, and if you have not taken a whirl on the Salt and Pepper whirl-i-gig ride on the midway, and shrugged away the ever-present discomfiting sight of rusty support struts shored up by weathered wood, and instead trusted your own bodily future to the guy gripping the brake lever on the ride, and if you have not done all this and listened to the sound of distant happy screams pinging through the steamy August night, occasional warm breezes bringing in smoke from the barbecue chicken pit-seared by the volunteer fire department alongside the crescendo of motor power from the tractor pull or the demolition derby, you might not get how what I am saying is that all of this is fun and wholesome, not in a marmish way but in a manner that indicates the rightness of the festival and spectacle, which of course also clashes with the sense that much is not right under the surface, or at least complicated in a way that, once again, explains a lot of what pundits, paid gobs of money to explain, cannot explain.

About Trump. And rural America. And the politics of resentment that might not be exactly that even though they are that. And the veneer of rural nostalgic wholesomeness that is very much not the wholesomeness I mean. Because purity or truth or nostalgia or honor or consistency or fairness are all relative terms, each of them boxing you in when, instead, you really, really, really want to be on that Ferris wheel with that beaux/beau and the blanket and the hat and the funnel cake, high up over the crowd, where you can point to the people who are coming to the county fair in the way David Foster Wallace went to the Illinois State Fair, to pare his fingernails on the page and pretend to love it while also making it very clear that he has immense disdain for it, because he has immense desire to separate himself from his origins. You can point to them and say, *that person has never once thought about what it's like to actually live this life.*

I am saying, really, that DFW never, in fact, slept in the goat barn, which was actually a tent the year we did, when I was maybe eleven years old. We were in a tent because the Fair Board hadn't quite figured out where to stash the goats, so they made us share space with the chickens, probably because the chicken farmers didn't care or, moreover, because chicken farmers aren't really a thing. As specialists, I mean. You don't define yourself at the county fair as a chicken farmer. Chickens are a sidelight or a hobby. You might be proud of the giant flouncy head of your Polish crested chicken, or the compact prideful solidity of your bantam, or the absolute prototypical perfection of your Leghorn, but generally none of these chickens is your *thing*. No, you're a dairy farmer, or a goat farmer, or a sheep farmer, or a draft horse aficionado—which usually means you are a codger, and a legit old school farmer, with Amish neighbors.

If you have a chicken at the fair, you are not, it is safe to say, a riding horse person, an *equestrian*. Because that's a whole different breed of not-exactly-a-farmer, leather and wealth and horses stored in neat stables instead of grungy barns, and an attitude of removal that will be deeply, deeply wounded the next year, when the goats are given half of the aloof riding horse barn, and you are required by force of principle to refuse the convenience of the new door cut in the middle of the barn when you take your steeds out for a canter in the ring and, instead, slowly waltz the long way down the barn right through the goats or, rather, through the goat farmers or, more, the goat farmers' children who are showing the goats, so the goatish interlopers are forced to scurry to the sides of the stalls and make way for your regal insulted passage.

You can imagine the impact all of this has, politically? Can't you?

*   *   *

At the fair, my sister led the Pygmies again and again into the ring, where they trailed the circles of dairy goats like tiny periods at the ends of ungainly, awkwardly ostentatious sentences declaring Grand Champions and Best in Breed. Then, the most prestigious competition began: determining the year's Best Udder.

The animals moved into the ring, sprightly sashays, high heads, and tails pointed in the air. Beneath the hindquarters of each goat, the pendulous objects of examination bounced with each step. This held my eleven-year-old attention, the equally wholesome and furtive sight of girls and women dressed from head to toe in dairy whites, leading goats to be handled and judged with a limited and single-minded focus, a sorting not unlike that which would occur to me as the central concern of my junior high life in only a few years. Later, the resonance between goat and human would eventually dawn on me in a startling recognition of a different sort of goatiness, one far less wholesome, far more furtive, and far more troubling than a dozen does parading in a circle of sawdust under the gaze of a frowning, weathered judge. How odd a prim farm childhood, where the enterprise depends wholly on the production of sex, contained always to the barn, pert does tormenting our always-isolated buck, who bleated and licked the air, waiting for those rare moments when he could enjoy his release. Mostly, we avoided him, and focused our eyes on the swelling bellies of the does and appreciated the docility of my wether.

The judge watched the animals walk the circle, her eye trained to measure the standards of the American Dairy Goat Association, which favor "an attractive framework with femininity, strength, upstandingness, length, and smoothness of blending." The doe should be "strong yet refined" with "clean bone structure, showing freedom from coarseness." Her skin should be "thin, loose, and pliable with soft, lustrous hair." Judges are encouraged to watch for a "pleasing carriage and smoothness of walk." Later, the guidelines for my wether would focus on different attributes, points earned for animals that are "tractable" and "responsive" and "trusting" and "cooperative."

The goats moved, the dairy whites, the pleasing carriages coming to a halt as the judge pointed. She bent and fingered the teats, palpated the pink flesh of udders. She selected the preliminary order, the dairy goats at the head of the judging, the Pygmy still tailing behind. A glance beneath the line revealed the justness of this decision, the heavy udders of the leaders showing off impressive, if crude, mastery. The Pygmy had no chance.

Then, someone displeased with the sorting called for a *milk off.*

The barn sprung to action, my mother alongside the others hustling into the ring carrying buckets. While my sister steadied her goat, my mother kneeled, first shaking the udder to stimulate lactation, then grabbing each teat, a pinch and a pull, until the sound of milk striking galvanized metal. The buckets frothed, and the unmistakable odor of warm sweetness mixed with sawdust and dung.

The dairy goat herders had a trick, long practiced, of denying their does the relief of morning milking. Instead, they allowed the animals to engorge, heavy production distending their udders. Now, those udders flopped, wrinkled teats hanging low beneath lopsided bags. The judge regarded this new information and turned to the Pygmy, whose natural state is that of the perky, the small and firm and efficient and modest udder of an animal worth noticing but who refuses to bring notice to herself.

My mother left the ring, her white 4-H t-shirt tucked neatly into clean blue jeans, her small frame moving smoothly through the gate. I do not know whether it was she who called for the milk off, or if a disgruntled dairy goat farmer hoped for a favorable reordering. Either way, the judge directed my sister and her Pygmy to the head of the line, their new and final position, as Best Udder. The shamed dairy goat herders considered this affront.

*   *   *

"You might say a poem is a semicolon, a living semicolon," writes Mary Ruefle, "what connects the first line to the last, the act of keeping together that whose nature is to fly apart. Between the first and last lines there exists—a poem—and if it were not for the poem that intervenes, the first and last lines of a poem would not speak to each other."

The grammar of the county fair is the grammar of our lives is the politics of the nation.

It is foolish to hope. It is foolish to keep wishing on the same collapsed star, but very well. Let us be foolish. Let us sing until dawn arrives. Let us lead our goats into the ring, and stretch our metaphors, and demand the draining of distended udders, and accept that the deeply human foundation of politics relies and preys on our shared desire to avoid being exiled, to avoid feeling like freaks, to come out as victorious.

Politics reveals our flaws. Politics is a terrible mirror of uncomfortable resolution. Politics shares the essence of poetry. Each reflects truth, so we must prepare ourselves for painful reading.

*　*　*

Soon enough, the other dairy goat farmers started raising Pygmies themselves. This cannot be misread as generous or anything other than a manifestation of the desire to win. It is politics.

Nor can any of this can be conflated with a defense of the recent rural capacity for neofascism. Indeed, the politics of rural conservatism is abhorrent, an ugliness borne from a stew of rancid nostalgia, petty selfishness, the escalating influence of religious extremism, and the manipulative dark brilliance of political strategists who recognized the power of outrage.

The story I tell here, about the goats, and about the trophy my sister won, is also a story reinforcing exactly what that concocted outrage whispers: The outsiders won. The outsiders cheated by using the rules to expose a long-standing practice of sanctioned cheating.

But cheating, also, is not the right word, not at all. Cheating isn't even exactly the right word to describe the practice of the other farmers, who understood that if you just don't milk your goat, the udder fills, so it looks better, and that's not really cheating cheating. Because the judge can reorder things. Because the competitors can challenge. It's not cheating cheating in the same way a spit ball pitcher isn't cheating cheating. I mean, that's *cheating* but it's clever and cool and okay until you get caught, until your corked bat splits open or your pine tar-soaked hat is found to be just a little too sticky. Or your goat gets floppy and unstructured when milked out.

Or, better, you fashion some legislation in the Pennsylvania legislature that ends the practice of single-button straight ticket voting—which Democrats like because it helps them run up the score in urban Philly and Pittsburgh—or allows for universal mail-in voting, which as the GOP you like because senior citizens like voting by mail and you think they're your secret advantage. That's *legislation*, not cheating cheating, or it isn't until your desperate cult-president realizes he's going to lose the election and it will be easy to blame mail-in votes in advance because a pandemic has appeared and won't go away even when you deny it exists, and it turns out Democrats are a lot more likely to vote by mail, so *that* is something you can call cheating cheating, even though it isn't cheating at all. And calling not-cheating cheating is also, somehow, not cheating, politically, regardless of truth and consequence. And getting pissed when the Pennsylvania

Supreme Court calls not-cheating not-cheating, well, that might not be cheating but it also sounds familiar if you've spent time in the dusty ring of the county fair.

Because what I am saying is that roguish taking of advantage is a kind of cheating long tolerated in American folklore and practice. We only get mad, I suppose, when we don't realize the wide margin or gray area that can still count within the broad matrix of legit. That's not limited to the farm or the fair or the political area, and if you think otherwise just have a gander at your speedometer the next time you're barreling down the interstate. Or, say, ask your local congressperson, particularly if you live in a rural, conservative place, to define cheating.

*   *   *

Understanding the politics of a category we might loosely call rural Pennsylvania farmers, few of whom actually make a *living* farming, even those who are trying to make a living, has quite a bit to do with the other insults that descend upon the county fair.

Take, for example, my family, and our farm, and that year my mother introduced Pygmy goats into the mix at the county fair, into the mix of the dairy goat competition, in accordance with the specifically defined rules of the official Dairy Goat Association but not exactly in accordance with the long-standing practice of the scions of dairy goat show dominance in Indiana County, Pennsylvania. Take, as another example, our goat club being the only one, I am sure, deploying Robert's Rules and using the mechanism of the farm as a way to explore civic decorum. It is easy to think we were the odd ones.

I am writing about then, yes, but also about now. I was a boy showing goats at the county fair in the 1980s, heart of the Reagan years, in a conservative house already out of step with whatever "Republican" had and would come to describe. Not Lincoln. Not Eisenhower. Not even Nixon, really, other than the paranoia of circling enemies and an instability of civic faith that is mistaken as justification for secret tapes, or theories of conspiratorial cabals, or the engorgement of udders.

It's not that different, you see? Righteousness is stable entitlement, an order that never shifts away from you or, rather, can only shift if it shifts toward you.

Put another way, the permissive nature of what counts as cheating relies on a common order of ethics, thus the affront to justice is less about the cheating itself but, instead, about the wideness of the window of what we consider ethical as person, or a goat club, or a nation. It is far too easy to say *cheater* and be done with it. That gets us nowhere, of course. Like so much, there is no stability to the category of righteousness, and the moment we believe there is, we have already lost. Rather, the moment we begin to believe that cries for righteousness will solve the problems of the world is the moment we have forgotten how the word itself is constructed, a sawdust, dung and sour milk world of goats toddling around a ring, all of us caring a little too much about the winning instead of the community.

* * *

Nonetheless, the trophy remained on our family room mantle for years, a miniature replica milk can emblazoned with the words,

"Best Udder," and what I always thought was the narrow etching of a stylized chicken. Eventually, my mother explained this to me, also, that the sketch signaled the form of a goat's backside, tail in the air, udder hanging beneath. She referred to this as embarrassing, as pornographic, yet for years, the can remained.

At meetings, she leaned the posterboard "I move" sign against the trophy, the butting buck so close to the object of his desire, but forever stalled, never quite in motion enough to reach what he longed for. Propriety, though, mattered, whether he sought it or not. My mother dusted the can carefully, arranging it just so, angling it in the sunlight to greet each visitor to our home.

★ **SIX** ★

SPIRITUAL DANGERS

The family farmhouse sits near the bottom of the valley at the end of the road. The massive berm of the town's bypass route creates an unnatural ridge, a hundred-foot high privacy fence that blocks through traffic, television signals and, my father claimed, tornados.

On this latter point, we had clear evidence. Not long after buying the property from a bankrupt housing developer, he drove to the farm with my sister. Storms rattled the windows, and the sky must have turned green. Turning onto Twolick Drive, my father and my sister watched a funnel cloud drift overhead. At the farm, nothing had been touched. The tornado rode the terrain, lifted from the hillsides and floated past the decayed farmhouse that, really, would have been better off smashed.

For a year, my father drove out to the farm to make a home out of that house. Snakes lived inside, alongside rats, all of them unbothered by the fraternity brothers who had been the most recent human residents. Their beer cans lined the cracked basement floor, where beams of light cut through the loose rock foundation.

"Burn it down," my uncle suggested, looking at the house his older brother had joyfully bought. Let it be clear: It was a good deal. Let it also be clear: No one else wanted it.

When securing the mortgage, the local banker stared slack-jawed at the house my father wanted to finance. This was the main structure of the one hundred acre parcel, the hearth, the center. It was intended, also, as the financial backbone of the deal.

"I can't write a loan for this," the banker said. It was just too rough, worthless really. No doubt, he agreed with my uncle. Better to start with fresh earth than suffer the labors of an impossible rehab. Plow it under along with the overgrown fields. Then there would be something to work with.

But my father was adamant. He liked the feel of the place, and I think the challenge called to his soul. He refused to recognize the source of the melody, the sirens who wailed from within deteriorated plaster lath, who arced along the frayed cloth of knotted wiring, who slithered under the mounds of trash in the basement.

The banker just couldn't do it. The house offered no collateral, instead added liability. To write the loan, he looked toward the barn. The roof leaked, spiderwebs infested the ceilings, and the boards had long since weathered to gray. He nodded. Better than the house, and good enough for the bank.

* * *

Who knows, really, what happened that morning? October, first blushes of cold on the way. Me, walking the three blocks from my house to campus. Me, thinking about the cascading bullshittery of the past couple of years. A brain tumor, Brexit, the ascendency of Trump, and the fueling of almost too many outrages to enumerate. All of that in just 2016.

That fucker is running unopposed again, I muttered to myself. I remember that moment clearly, emerging in my head right before I stepped across College Street to campus. The *fucker* was the state rep, and we were two weeks from the 2018 elections.

Outrage, I think, stems from the sense that we ought to be better than we are. My own outrage is fueled by the complexity of love. This is my place, Western Pennsylvania always my realest home, yet it behaves badly. I might call it foolish optimism, then, that I stepped into my office and slapped an announcement onto Facebook. I'd run as a late write-in for the state house seat, an effort I knew could not succeed. But if I did well enough, I wrote, I'd run for real in 2020.

There. Now it's public. Now I had to follow through.

* * *

"So the artist as citizen, in *this* sense, is someone who through her creations is a contributor to the community—is, indeed, a catalyst for the transformation of community, real and imagined."

—Eric Liu, *Become America*

* * *

The rooster's name was Andropov.

This was the early 1980s when Ronald Reagan seemed to be on television every night, his face gathered in by the antenna rooted atop the tall pole behind the house. We had three channels, more or less, plus PBS, and that only counted when *Sesame Street* or *Mr. Rogers* was on. Reagan crackled through the television screen on every channel, no matter which direction the rotor spun our antenna.

Bzzz—thud.

The rotor dial hummed, static lifting to reveal only another version of his half-smile, my fellow Americans.

Bzzz—thud.

Outside, Andropov raged. There was no television in the chicken coop, and the rooster seemed oblivious to the momentum of history. He cared little about Reagan's future as Commie killer, did not worry about the Berlin Wall, and was unfazed by the weight of Hungary, Czechoslovakia, Poland.

Bzzz—thud.

He chased us, proud breast thrust into the air. His feet churned, striking the ground like a shoe against a dusty table. He ignored our yells, darted away from our kicks, came back with beak and attitude, one day cornering my mother, who took refuge, not for the last time, in a hay feeder.

Bzzz—thud.

Eventually, Andropov grew old. My father's hands forgave no past. The hatchet might as well have been guided by Reagan's own imperative. Andropov abdicated to the stock pot. The meat proved too tough to chew, so we fed the soup to the dogs.

* * *

"There are two spiritual dangers in not owning a farm. One is the danger of supposing that breakfast comes from the grocery, and the other that heat comes from the furnace."
——Aldo Leopold, *A Sand County Almanac*

* * *

Yes, I lost the write-in. Of course I did. But it went better than even I thought. This was 2018, when just trying seemed almost like enough. My campaign amounted to a series of Facebook videos outlining issues, my talking head on the screen explaining the ignored issues that doomed us. I recorded one of the first ones in my car outside the cancer center in suburban Pittsburgh, right after crawling out of the MRI tube. The machine's mechanical beats still echoed in my ears as I talked about healthcare, and how our own family suffered significant ongoing debt paying for my brain surgery, radiation, and annual follow-up MRIs even though our insurance would be described as "good."

I'm sure I decided to run for office because of my brain tumor. How can you not try out different pathways when mortality looms so clearly? This is either a brilliant or quixotic motivation.

Thus the campaign videos. And some door knocking. And a couple of invitations to speak to voters' groups. And the rebuffing of newspapers who label the effort too last minute to warrant coverage despite the evidence of interest based on Facebook shares and on-the-street moments of *Hey! You're that guy!*

* * *

Our sheep occupied the lower half of the barn. The flock was never enormous, maxing near fifty in ambitious years, and the ewes exhibited the placid blankness for which sheep are celebrated. Sheep live their lives in stupor and brief terror. Mostly, they mill around and bleat, but they panic when a farmer, say, bangs on a plastic chlorine bucket repurposed to carry oats.

Even then, sheep find it hard to hold a grudge. Inside the barn, the frothing flock hurtles toward the exit like a single fluffy organism. There, it faces the bottleneck of the sheep hatch, a trap door cut into the side of the barn with a chainsaw. Sheep climb aboard other sheep, shove heads deep into wool, clog the door like soggy cotton balls swirling down the drain. Outside, each sheep releases through the door and takes a few frenzied steps. Stupor returns in a wave three feet beyond the hatch.

Rams are different, driven by fury and a blend of machismo and Napoleon complex. Perhaps the burden of responsibility weighs heavily upon their thick necks. So many ewes, so many lambs, one ram.

That gives too much credit as rams exhibit the kind of blind, lurid stupidity only seen elsewhere in isolated environments: fraternity houses, spring break, academic conferences. Rams live only to prove themselves worthy of their position. Rams possess one single philosophy, centered entirely on self-image.

Charley was our ram, a squat, dingy Cheviot whose wool seemed always tinged with mud. While the ewes called out with soft, plaintive, almost lyric voice, Charley employed the sheep version of a Bronx accent. Low, bored, a threatening blat. He surveyed the flock and operated with clinical, diabolical haphazardness. Often, he ignored whoever waded among the flock casting feed. Sometimes, he became sentinel, announcing at the gate his plan of defense. At his worst, he lurked. He blended in among the ewes, swam beneath the taller Finns and Suffolk like a fuzzy, hardheaded piranha. He had strategy, some modicum of guile to augment unabashed passivity. He waited, watched, then streaked into peripheral vision as a knee-cap seeking missile.

After near misses, artful dodges, and an assortment of daring escapes, my mother finally ran afoul of the ram. He charged hard, 150 pounds of churning ire. She scampered into a hay feeder hung on the wall, safe but now cut off from escape. For an hour, Charley strutted back and forth. He dared her, talked smack, staked his claim to that space once and forever. My mother called out for help, growing angry and, no doubt, panicked. Charley had her, and there was nothing she could do.

Finally, my father heard the yells and executed a rescue. My father had grown tired of Charley's attitude. My father wore size fourteen steel-toed work boots.

For a ram, the charge precedes an expectation of impact. We've all seen that on the nature shows: Majestic Bighorns rear back, clash skulls, repeat. It's how you sort it out. Charley streaked forward, and my father raised one size fourteen into the air. In that clash, when steel and leather met bone and wool, lay

the epic of the pastures. Two rams now, one a tired old alpha protecting his human flock; the other a frenzied maniac unused to
gauging size. There was impact, a thud, the force of the ram
driven straight back into his own skull.

Stunned, Charley shuttled backward. He considered the
fluke, weighed his options, and charged the boot again. Dazed
now, Charley refused to submit. He gave it a third charge,
manure flicking in the air under his whirling hooves.

As my father tells the story, this final strike changed everything. Charley felt the unyielding force of steel, could not shake
the cobwebs from his now reeling skull. He bleated, something
about anytime anywhere, then retreated into the flock, never to
challenge my father again.

*   *   *

I lost.

But the first rough official tabulations showed me receiving
851 votes. The next Monday, I went to the courthouse to review
the official voting books and found almost a hundred more,
write-ins listed for Matt Terrance and, Michael Ferrence, and
Matthew Fetterman (a voter apparently confusing me with John
Fetterman, on the ballot that year for Lt. Governor), and That
Guy Whose Name Starts With F, as well as The Guy on Facebook Ask (name redacted), as well as a litany of close-but-no-
cigar last names coupled with Matt or Matthew: Ferrer, Ferraro,
Fetter, Farreah, Ferrenc, Ferrous, Ferris, Ferentz, Ferrick, and
DeFerence. Fourteen votes came in for me in neighboring state
districts, along with four votes for the US House.

I beat a slew of other write-ins who received a single vote or two, tough competitors like Stephen Colbert, Anyone But Him, Anyone Else, Jesus, God, and Red Breasted Nuthatch.

All of which means I lost *badly*.

Which also means I pulled in more than 5 percent of the vote in two weeks, unfunded, spending zero dollars, just through word of mouth.

It felt like momentum. It felt like, in fact it was, the beginning of my 2020 campaign.

*   *   *

Eric Liu writes in *Become America*, "The United States has a creed, contained in foundational documents and given life in fateful collective acts. Devotion to that creed—and the mystic memory of such devotion—is what makes us American."

Liu writes in the wake of 2016, after the devastating shockwave that shattered the myth of our national honor. He took to delivering a series of "civic sermons," traveling the country to gather folks together in common practice. Here, he believed, we could rekindle the embers.

The book is hopeful, and inspiring, even as some of its promise became fast wreckage. Liu visited Glenn Beck, for example. He writes of the meeting, how he found surprising connection. "He wants to learn from me—from you—and others on the left," Liu writes. "He wants to disagree with me in a way that everyone else can learn from: with respect and genuine openness."

These sentences do not make sense even if they might have in the moment Liu wrote them. Glenn Beck returned to the brand of Glenn Beck, carrying water for Donald Trump, for right wing demagoguery, whatever it takes to keep the dollars rolling in, I guess. A brand is a brand.

Still, I hear the resonance of Liu. "The point of civic life in this country is not to avoid such tensions. Nor is it for one side to achieve 'final' victory," he writes. It is about hard conversations and disagreements and full engagement with the problems that are now so clearly in the open. "The point is for us all to wrestle perpetually with these polarities, to fashion hybrid solutions that work for the times . . . then to start again."

It's odd, now, to think about the optimism of the early years of MAGA, when you could almost pretend conversation was enough. When we admitted, in some quarters, that ignoring right-wing anger was a source of its power. When we recognized that denial allows injury to fester. When it seemed like frank conversations might be enough.

*　*　*

Before the county fair, my father had t-shirts made. Yellow cotton embellished with red felt: Cardinal Creek Farm. He assigned titles for each of us, arced beneath the farm's name in the same red felt.

He was "foreman," my mother "manager," my brother "shepherd," my sister "goatherder." I was the youngest, still little and perpetually uninterested in the farm. I was "water boy."

We took to the barn as a family to round up the sheep. My father backed the pickup to the edge of the paddock, and my brother leaned a wooden ramp against the tailgate. Together, the rest of my family led a stream of calm sheep into the truck.

One ewe, an old matron, panicked. She stampeded, slicked out of the way when my brother tried to squeeze his arms around her neck. She slowed, caught her breath, then took off again when someone else came near.

I squared my body, digging my sneakers into the dried horse manure beneath my feet. She was headed my way, that old ewe, and I sensed my chance. My eight-year-old mind understood the alchemy of promotion. Catch that ewe, get a new title. I wanted to be helpful.

She approached. I can still see her black head, the dull eyes with rectangular pupils. The rest I remember as flashes.

The sheep.

The belly of the sheep.

The ceiling of the barn.

The ceiling distorted by tears.

My family couldn't stifle the laughter. Someone pointed to my shirt, perfect muddy sheep tracks striping the center of my chest.

* * *

"When traces of blood begin to mark your trail you'll see something, maybe. Probably not."

—Edward Abbey, *Desert Solitaire*

* * *

My father honed the shears to razor edges. My sister handled them like an artist, pinching the metal just so, not too tight, or close, or fast, or slow. The caked, brown edges of the sheep dropped into a growing pile of dingy wool. In such fashion, she sculpted the sheep to Davidian ideal.

Close-cropped, fresh-white, lanolin-slick, taut-muscled, prize-winning sheep.

The sheep cared little for aesthetics, cared less for the pinching whine of the shear's jaws. It kicked, sideways, sudden. The shears arced upward, then down. Like nothing, barely a pinch, they slid into Jeanine's bare ankle. They drove an inch straight down until they caught on bone. Yes, they were sharp.

My brother pulled them out, and my sister limped into the house, spurting a cardinal trail of bloody footsteps along the flagstone walk.

This was her most lasting prize, a permanent scar on her ankle that outlived the giant pink Reserve Grand Champion ribbons that waited at the fairgrounds.

* * *

From a window high above the city, Yuri Andropov could have watched Soviet troops subdue Budapest. Andropov served as the Soviet ambassador to Hungary, a position that seems redundant or, perhaps, historically dishonest. How does an ambassador function within a figurehead state, itself only nominally its own?

When trouble began to mount, the Hungarians staking a claim for themselves and their nation, the Red Army rolled. Even as they approached, wily or deceived Andropov assured Hungary's leader, Imre Nagy, that violence would be avoided.

Thousands died in the bloodbath, including Nagy, executed for treason.

Andropov ascended to direct the KGB, then took the mantel of General Secretary for the Communist Party of the Soviet Union in 1982 after the death of his predecessor, Leonid Brezhnev. Andropov died after serving a little more than a year, then was replaced by Konstantin Chernenko, who also died in office after little more than a year.

The infirmity of old men opened the office for Mikhail Gorbachev, who began unprecedented peace talks with Ronald Reagan, released the Eastern Bloc from effective Soviet control and, in the end, oversaw the end of the Soviet Union.

Hungary, crushed in 1956 while its ambassador watched, finally became an independent democratic state in 1989.

* * *

In 2020, I lost every precinct in the district except for two. I lost in the city of Meadville, considered a Democratic "stronghold," since it is the only place in Crawford County where Democrats outnumber Republicans. The margin of advantage is tiny, and there are still more non-Democrats in Meadville than Democrats once you count up the Libertarians and independents, the latter of whom tend to find the GOP and the Libertarians slightly too progressive for their tastes.

I know I lost everywhere because the reelected state representative gloated on his Facebook page, rubbing salt in the wound, grinding his heel in my face, taking a victory lap after winning a race he started with a 30 percent registration advantage.

*   *   *

Each year, my father bought a pair of feeder calves for the freezer. For a few months, they roamed the pasture and grew on a diet of grass, transforming from gawky, wobbled youngsters to full-on steers. They lived their last month as gourmands, gorging themselves on ground field corn and hay. The corn fattened them more quickly than grass, softened their muscles and added striations of fat. From the beginning, these cows were steak.

As with all farm animals, the final loading proves difficult. The truck arrived. One steer bolted for the paddock. My brother darted to swing the rear gate shut. The startled steer tried to change direction, stumbled, and a half ton of USS Bollocks ran aground, pinning my brother behind the gate.

The steer snorted away, and my brother swayed out. From the distance, I examined his shirt for track marks, just in case I could make fun.

*   *   *

"There comes a moment when the image of our life parts company with the life itself, stands free, and, little by little, begins to rule us."
                    —Milan Kundera, *The Art of the Novel*

*   *   *

On the farm, while my father worked to ready the house, I played. I was too little to do much more than wander like Thoreau—squish around the banks of the swampy pond, scuff through piles of construction dirt, climb up the barn gate. There,

I liked to show off. Let go, fall back, then catch the wood at the last second. A playmate raised the stakes. He shook the gate, and I fell.

My elbow banged hard into the concrete paddock threshold. My father scooped me into his pickup truck, drove me to the hospital for X-rays, anesthesia, and the first of three plaster casts I'd eventually earn on the farm.

*　*　*

I needed a farm identity, so I got a pig. I'm not really sure why, nor whose idea it was. I imagine it was a youngest child's conscious but now forgotten effort to do something different, at least. A pig is not a sheep, nor a goat, nor a chicken, nor a cow, nor a horse. A pig was mine.

Skywise came tiny, just a young piglet. Every morning, I slipped rubber boots over my bare feet and walked out to the barn in my pajamas to feed him. He greeted breakfast with enthusiasm and, frankly, charm. He knew me, which isn't surprising for a pig. They're smart, much more so than goats, sheep, even horses. Pigs get a bad rap for dirtiness, but once you know a pig, even love a pig, you understand something fundamental about the nature of sorrow and intelligence.

He grew, as this is the mission of pigs. He came to me at one and a half feet, all snout and baby fat, easy to lift. Within six months, he outweighed me by a hundred pounds. But the time came, as it always must on the farm. I went to school, aware that my pig would not be there when I came home. My parents went out to the barn to lead him onto the butcher's truck.

His panic, perhaps, is the truest sign of his wisdom. He startled, refused to go where he was destined to end. I don't know if the butcher frightened him, tried to manhandle him in a way Skywise was not accustomed. But he simply would not get on the truck. Maybe he knew, and I worry now that my pig sensed betrayal.

My father stepped in. The pig was in full flight, however, and even this familiar person could not settle him. He charged or simply tried to evade capture, driving two hundred pounds of pig into my father's right knee. It buckled, and the bones separated at the joint. My father collapsed to the ground. He lay in pig shit, unable to stand by himself. My pig retreated into the corner of the pen.

My mother snapped my father's knee back into place, helped her husband rise. They herded the pig into the truck without further incident. My father showered, put on a tie, went to work and lectured to his biology students, perhaps about Aldo Leopold.

★  ★

VIOLENCE

I.

I am in high school. It is May, a blessed half day. My friends and I sit at a pizza joint for lunch. We are band kids and swimmers, good students. Seniors.

Another group sits behind us, underclassmen, football jocks. Among them is a class clown who deploys the pull-out-the-chair trick on a backup linebacker. The linebacker falls on his ass, which we don't see. His drink spills on top of him, which we also don't see.

But we hear the laughter, turn to view the linebacker haul himself from the ground. The class clown can't hold back. This is all just so flat out hilarious. The air shifts. The linebacker cold-cocks the class clown, who collapses in a heap.

The shock of silence. The aversions of gazes. My friend Andy standing beside me.

"That's not right," he says. And the linebacker threatens him. And Andy again, "That's not right."

Things settle. No more punches are thrown. The class clown fetches the linebacker a new drink. Andy sits back down, mutters that none of us stood with him, which is true.

*   *   *

I think about the pizza house punch often. I think it has a lot to do with why I ran for office. I thought about Andy often while campaigning, the courage of his standing and the cowardice of the rest of us.

I think, most of all, about my own fear. I was not ready, then, to take a punch, literal or figuratively.

*   *   *

Throughout the election season of 2020, a jacked-up pickup truck exhaust-bombed the College every afternoon. Main Street runs through the middle of campus, an orientation that stops traffic every hour as students stream across the road.

Maybe that was the truck's protest as it revved through campus, twin stacks breaking the quiet and rolling coal. Probably not. The protest was a threat, which spawned conversations and suspicions with colleagues about the concern of shit going bad after the election, how we all expected it in some way as autumn arrived. We worried campus would be vulnerable. A target. The College itself told us they had a security plan in the works, just in case.

I wish I could dismiss our fear as paranoia, but at some level, the roaring of a truck's exhaust was intended to remind us all of the risk of standing up. It meant to stoke the fear of calling attention to ourselves. It confirmed our fear that violence would be the consequence of breaking the local social order.

* * *

The fundamental vocabulary of politics is steeped in violence.

Political campaigns have "war chests" and "war rooms."

Metaphors teach us how to make sense of the world, which is itself a mysterious panoply of electric impulse and light. Metaphors teach us how to approach experience, and the language of politics has grown ever more violent.

When everything is pitched battle, when words themselves are sharpened and packed with gunpowder, we are preparing ourselves for further violence.

* * *

Violence is embedded in our sense of self, of what we call triumph, of how we see *fierce* as a marker of pride, of who we include and exclude, and how dented doors and broken windows and late-night shouting street arguments are not an aberration of the violence we endure and commit in rural America.

This is what is from here, what stays here, what we make when we decide we are fine with the perpetual violence, personal and communal, that marks our days.

Let me put it this way: Autumn brings us both Election Day and the culmination of high school football season. Fortunes are defined.

* * *

The poet James Wright writes in "Autumn Begins in Martins Ferry, Ohio," about football and poverty and rage and the abandonment of the Ohio River Valley, itself not far from where I live:

> Therefore,
> Their sons grow suicidally beautiful
> At the beginning of October,
> And gallop terribly against each other's bodies.

* * *

When I was in junior high, playing saxophone in the marching band, sitting in the stands on a Friday night like every fall Friday night, I watched the field with the rest of the hushed crowd while the ambulance rolled onto the grass, and the paramedics cut the jersey off a boy who sat in my homeroom, and they hauled him away, and he was in school the next day laughing that it was just a cracked rib.

II.

Lately, friends have opened serious conversations about learning to shoot guns. For the first time in their lives, they recognize a version of the fevered urgency that animates gun-fetish 2A radicals. When your daily experience is awash in threats of violence, it is perhaps natural to think about having your own violent response. This is, after all, more or less the entire marketing ploy of both the NRA and the GOP.

Since I grew up on a farm shooting groundhogs, and since I worked as the shooting sports director of a Boy Scout camp after college, and since I am identified by my friends as some kind of semiredeemed Appalachian hillbilly, partly because I used to drive a pickup truck and mostly because people not from rural places aren't really quite sure what being an Appalachian means and slip far too easily into easy cliché misunderstandings, they ask me about guns.

Of course, it is true that I know how to shoot guns, and I have shot them, and I have killed animals and eaten them, and I have generally participated in a rural culture alien and sometimes disturbing to folks who did not grow up in places where a skinned deer hanging from the backyard walnut tree is no big deal.

So far, I have not showed any of these friends how to shoot. I do not, in fact, own any guns. Not at the moment.

During my campaign, however, I thought about asking my father for one of my old guns. When the white supremacists started paying attention to me online, when the general threats that sadly come with the territory of being a rural Democrat started feeling real, I wondered if I should retrieve my .30–40 Krag, just in case.

* * *

The boy who was punched was like us: scrawny, maybe a little gawky, funny. He wasn't a jock himself though he was on the football team. Later, he'd start acting in school plays, and if the sorting of high schools had more flexibility, he would have been sitting with us.

But he wasn't sitting with us. In fact, he was out of place, or maybe just didn't quite understand his place. He'd fashioned a fit, I guess. Class clown, jester, the funny jock who wasn't really a jock. At the pizza joint, he miscalculated. Maybe a half-day giddiness got the best of him.

I remember the hush, that moment when the air changes. A pause. No one quite knows what has happened or what will. Let's leave it there for a moment: a linebacker sitting on the floor, a paper cup of cheap pizza joint pop frozen in flight. A cascade of liquid and ice. The face of the linebacker is a shocked grimace, then slowly narrowed to anger. The class clown is gleeful, lightness still flickering in his eyes at the moment the frame speeds back to life.

One punch. A slapping noise, really, less resonant than what you hear in movies. The class clown is on the floor, holding his jaw. The linebacker stands over him, wide hipped and solid. Cocked for another, if he needs it.

"That's not right," Andy says, standing too.

I don't remember the act of his standing, but for thirty years I have seen him standing tall. He was a solid boy, tall and muscled and quick to flash anger. He faces the table of jocks. The rest of us look at our pizza.

"That's not right," Andy says again.

*   *   *

We carry the wounds of high school with us forever.

There's nothing brilliant in that statement because we've all gone through it. Our bodies and minds shift from kid to not-kid while expectations of our future gather around us. The alleged grown-ups of our lives apply the pressure of social order, voiced as anxieties about permanent records or getting into a good college or getting a good job or getting through whatever phase has become the mode of cultural panic.

Adolescence carries so much weight. Too much. You never want to be the freak, and you almost always feel like you are.

Sometimes our personal freakishness leads to garden variety hurt, the kind that helps us grow. Sometimes the hurt is deep and lasting. Except it isn't the freakishness that hurts. It's the discipline against freakishness, the atmosphere of threat and exposure. Again, I offer no deep wisdom. We all went to high school.

We also all live the rest of our lives in the wake of high school, which likely created foundational cracks that make it impossible to get the roofline of our adultness to fully square up. So we keep trying over and over again to fix an amorphous flaw, return to moments without knowing we're doing it, and try to walk in a different direction.

But what did Thoreau say, about paths? About how quickly he'd worn one in the grass outside his shack? Our habit, maybe even instinct, is to repeat the paths we know. That means we spend our lives witnessing the reverberating storms of adolescent anger, always facing the choice to sit or stand up when someone gets punched in the face for breaking the unwritten codes of social hierarchy.

III.

I consider, now, the shared paths between my state rep and me. Catholic kids. Small town kids. Rural kids. Kids who maybe didn't go far enough away for college. Kids who probably both worried about catching the eye of bullies.

My state rep is a dark mirror, an anti-me as much as I am an anti-him. He hates poets, and I am a writer. He attacks teachers, and I a professor. He rails against funding things he sees as frivolous. I rail against the inhumane nature of spending priorities that allow poverty to flourish.

The hardest truth: I see my state rep, and I understand my state rep, because I have known my state rep all my life, and I could have easily become the same kind of person. It's a frightening admission, considering the narrow margins between right wing zealot and not: different dominance, different group, different high school balance, different parents. I was lucky.

I grew up as a socially conservative Catholic kid in a rural high school. I remember answering "Ronald Reagan" when our civics teacher asked which US presidents could be defined as truly great. I remember the teacher chuckling, saying "maybe," but leaving it at that.

I know better now, and I should have understood better then, but I did not. It's hard to understand the gravity of rural conservatism when you're a kid, particularly when the historic righteousness of Republicanism sticks to its contemporary soullessness.

My friends all left town for college, to places that count as prestigious. I stayed home at the state university, because it was free, and because I was afraid to leave, and because I have always loved where I am from even when I hate it. Maybe I have always sensed, and therefore refused, the bullshit narratives of rural America that your only chance comes if you leave it. We are hollowed by these departures. We're left with the dynamics of our learned violence, and those who stay face a difficult choice. Do we throw down with the people who favor the system we've got, that works only for a few? Or do we work to build a different world?

I mean this in a generous way: Politicians like my state rep legislate in a way they believe will save their communities. They are wrong but they—how do you really say this?—mean well. They do. They think they understand the nation and themselves, even though their actions are almost always described by their role as puncher or punched. They are either bully or victim to a bully.

I cannot pretend to see any goodness in their sort of political philosophy because such politicians, and such voters, are blinded by the sirens of American economic violence. So many of us have been harmed by the dynamics of the American economy, and instead of fighting to rework that system, so many wind up simply trying to get on the winning side of harm.

They wobble up after being punched and fetch a new pop for the puncher. Too many spend their lives tearing down the same people their own bullies tear down, and too many elected officials spend their days figuring out how to stay on their bullies' good sides. I cannot imagine a more miserable curse. But I also understand how easy it would be to accept it as your fate.

*   *   *

We act on our wounds. That's how narratives work, on the pages of a novel and in our lives. High school wounds us all. I joke about that with my writing students often, that now's the time to refashion the hurt. Write the wounds. Rewrite them. Use them to imagine different outcomes, to assess how our wounds can lead to certain ways of thinking, that we need not accept our ongoing harm as inevitable. I share with my students what I see as a beautiful truth, that writing gives us a chance to reshape the trajectory of our wounding. We don't have to stay in the path offered to us.

*   *   *

High schools shape American culture, too much, and this is politics at work. We fetishize the experience on film, on the page, and in our shared sense of what it means to be an American. This shape has an even greater power in rural America, where high schools often become the center of all social and cultural expression. It's where you go on Friday night, your entire life. It's where you find your sense of identity forever. If you want to know the power dynamic of any local politics, look at who ranks at the top of the heap in the local high schools.

Because the glory of high school is written in violence. I mean that literally. High school is the place where we learn to sort ourselves to the standard of violence. Swaggers and pickup trucks. An eye always searching for threat, perceived or otherwise. *You wanna go?*, the prevailing question of our hallways, the preening chest-pumping question one dude offers another, sometimes in jest, often not, fists balled up.

Our champions are those who withstand pain, and even more, those who inflict it. We learn to accept the legacy of pain handed to us, and we are taught that no one should complain about the pain they experience. Be tough. That has political implications. Cultural ones. Personal ones. High school is where we learn to submit our bodies to the purposes of economy and fight like hell to make sure that never changes. Rarely do we stand against it, risking our own chin in declaring what is not right.

Try looking at your own politicians through the lens of high school social order. I bet you see something. Try looking at the momentum of MAGA, the devotion to Trump, the now-overt hatred that consumes the GOP and is metastasizing from rural America to all of it, and think about how high school prepared us to accept this. January 6 was, in a sense, akin to the ritualized violence of a high school pep rally. Only it was real, and terrifying, and a threat to the democratic stability Americans take as permanent and unshakeable.

IV.

Rage is our directed violence. And in high school, we learn to rage. We learn the value of it, the way other boys cower at those who have the rage. We sort ourselves not through what we offer to others but in how we can preserve ourselves in the face of the ever-present threat of violence. Maybe we become the class clown, who makes the mistake of pulling out the wrong chair, and we receive the decking we have been trained to accept as our due. Maybe we become the troubled, violent, scared jock, who has to throw the punch if he wants to maintain status as empowered. Maybe we run for school board and decide to ban books that dream a different world into existence because we are afraid to accept the reality of violence inflicted upon us, the violence of limitation, of atrophied imagination, the violence that turned us into fleshy vessels of bigotry and hatred.

In high school, we learn that violence and the consumption of bodies is our purpose in life. I don't exaggerate. This is high school in the Rust Belt and Appalachia and the Midwest and the Northeast and across rural America. In high school, we learn it is better to punch first.

V.

A different way, perhaps, can be found in places like Ross Gay's remarkable book of "essayettes," *The Book of Delights*. Gay describes his writing of this book as a practice of developing "a kind of delight radar. Or maybe it was more like the development of a delight muscle. Something that implies that the more you study delight, the more delight there is to study."

Few essays have struck me more powerfully than these. *The Book of Delights* is a masterfully casual book, honed with structural brilliance that seems like a series of off-the-cuff knock-you-on-your-ass observations about the delight of being. It arrived in 2019, in the middle of our Trumpian nightmare, exactly when we needed it and precisely when I wasn't ready to recognize how to leverage delight into the realm of, say, a candidacy.

Maybe, I admit, a political candidacy can never be delightful. Maybe politics itself is doomed for the muck. Or, rather, maybe campaigning has become so consumed by the muck that a delightful candidate can never rise above the mire. I am not, to be clear, calling myself delightful.

* * *

I resent the hatred that has blossomed inside of me. I hate the despair and sense of inevitable doom that is the lasting residue of my campaign. I want to be positive, and I want to tell you it will be okay. I want to tell you that if we keep trying, things will get better. But right now, I do not believe that.

* * *

I don't remember who said it, though I wish I could because they deserve credit, but someone recently explained how they recognized despair as a comforting laziness. It's easier to be angry than not. It feels better to be disillusioned at the daily drip of political fury than to do the harder work of finding shards of hope among that broken glass.

Maybe this is, for me, a turning point even though I am suspicious of hope these days. Things are bad, and it is far too easy to ignore the bad and call that hope.

We need antidotes, and I doubt those will be found in politics. Certainly, they will not be found in the strategizing of politicians, who always seek the easiest pathways. We get what we already have in politics, which is governed by the powerful inertia of the status quo. Violence is easy and familiar. Hope is difficult and foreign.

* * *

James Wright, then, writes about politics, too. He describes how we learn to destroy ourselves. He describes how that seems to matter, how personal destruction might yield mutual salvation or, rather, that we are conditioned to act as if it does.

Therefore, Wright could have written: At the beginning of November we gallop terribly against each other, ashamed to imagine a world better than the one we've been given.

This has nothing to do with high school, or maybe it does.

This has nothing to do with the pizza joint punch, or maybe it does.

This has nothing to do with poetry as an antidote to violence.

Or, conversely, poetry is everything.

*   *   *

The poetry of my corner of rural America:

The VP of the Allegheny College Dems, a trans woman who writes beautiful stories and thinks more deeply than almost anyone I know, who volunteered her time at the downtown Democratic HQ, even though walking there meant she'd be cat-called by leering assholes on the way.

The high school girl who organized a local Black Lives Matter march, who led us as the pickup trucks circled, coal-rolling our quiet protest, who kept us together when the jeering asshole shouted "all lives matter" while we lay silent in Meadville's central Diamond for the same amount of time George Floyd could not breathe.

The hundred folks who showed up to a political meet-and-greet in February, before Covid shut down in-person campaigning, who opened their checkbooks to help the fight against right-wing domination. And the hundred who showed up to an Erie backyard at the end of summer once we could gather again. And the fifty who showed up in the sweltering bay of a local tool and die shop in Meadville. Each of them declaring, through their presence, the validity of their claim to exist right here. Each of them demanding better than what we're given.

The gender-fluid local medium who lingered after one of my online town hall events to ask questions about how I successfully curled my mustache. Good wax is the answer, and that's poetry itself.

The Black preacher who invited me into his house when I was gathering candidacy petitions, interrupting his own Sunday family dinner to pour me a giant mug of coffee in one of his to-go cups because it was cold outside. Very.

The high school English teacher, in a neighboring school district, who stood up to her homophobic board by standing up for her LGBTQ+ students who were being told, through policy, that they don't matter. She paid the price, took heat from neighbors and the board, until her job was no longer tenable, maybe not even safe. But she took the punches, and kept standing up. "These kids," she told me in a message, "they deserve better, and they know it." They're the reason she has hope for the future.

Those kids.

The old codger lift operator at a local ski hill, where our older son was taking snowboard lessons, who pulled a mitten off his own hand because he noticed I'd lost one of mine, and how it is really actually true the people of northwestern Pennsylvania, like people all across rural America, will literally give you the shirt (mitten) off their own backs (hands).

These are delights and joys and signs of hope even when the hope itself feels thin. This is our hardest work, I think, the cultivation of the muscles of delight. I mean this politically. When so many of us suffer, and when so many of us can so easily fall prey to the easiest mechanisms of fear-mongering political action, and when so many of us fear the repetition of the learned violence of our lives, it seems impossible to risk beauty and hope.

We must risk it anyway. Beauty is our only hope. It's easy to be angry. It's easy to feel the siren song of hatred and despair. But we must never give up our goodness, which is embedded in the poetry of our presence here in rural America.

* * *

A writing exercise:

1. Describe your high school self.

2. Describe the dominant group of your high school.

3. Describe the dominant politics of your hometown.

4. Write a letter to this younger version of yourself. Tell them what life can be. Tell them the dreams they are allowed to have. Tell them they should never give up on goodness.

5. Never give up on goodness.

EIGHT

CROWN VETCH

Behind the parking lot of a local restoration seed company, a field of tall wildflowers buzzed. Insects winged from bloom to bloom, and the air was filled with Pennsylvania's August soundtrack: katydids, crickets, cicada, songbirds. In front of us, tractors and other heavy equipment moved between the warehouses and grain elevators, ushering seed that had become product, bagged and shipped and ready for sale.

I stepped forward to mingle with a group of local farmers waiting for the kickoff of the annual Crawford County Farm Bureau's Legislative Tour. Around me were members of the Bureau, all of whom try to make a living growing grain, or raising beef cattle, or milking cows, or nurturing bees. I could claim neither membership to the Bureau, nor a legislative position, but had finagled an invitation from this seed company's owner, somewhat accidentally. I'd sent him a letter asking if he'd support my candidacy even though I knew he was active in conservative political circles. But since he ran a conservation seed company and I am pro-conservation, I saw in his company the sort of rational, sensible environmental awareness I hoped to champion in Harrisburg. He responded by inviting me to the event.

As we waited, I chatted amicably with a local beef farmer. The usual stuff. About the nature of work on a farm. About my own childhood raising animals and showing goats at the county fair. I spoke the language of the farm, and she was genuinely friendly. Nonetheless, she could barely contain her amusement when I got around to mentioning why I was there.

"Oh, we love Brad," she said, then chuckled, after I told her I was running for state representative.

A moment later, Brad himself showed up in full political mode. He shook hands and said hello to the farmers, exchanged pleasantries. Everyone knew him. They were his people, neighbors and mostly GOP stalwarts. So, I relish the startled look in his eyes when he careened over, unaware, to introduce himself and shake my hand. He hadn't expected me there. On his turf.

Soon after, we boarded a school bus to tour the fields. The owner pointed to crop asters, and sunflowers, and lots of switchgrass. He talked of deer, and good hunting. He explained how most of the 9,000 acres they cultivate had been considered valueless junk land, too depleted to grow anything. It's doing well, now, since it's been converted to native plants and grasses. There's a lesson in that, he said.

The owner talked about promising markets opening up for wildflowers, grasses, and natives in general. Asters were perfect as ground cover underneath solar panels, and solar panels offer a stable income for questionable farmland. All of this could help a lot of farmers in struggling places. I recognized his pitch as essentially a defense of the merits of green development, even though I was riding a bus full of people who sneer at concepts like the Green New Deal. It would ruin them, they'd likely argue.

The bus passed the old family farmhouse. The owner's adult son lives there now and runs the day-to-day operations of the company. A giant Donald Trump sign fluttered in the late summer breeze. Contradictions. Deep-seated beliefs that connect not at all with other deep-seated beliefs.

* * *

When I became a candidate for the Pennsylvania House, I arrived carrying the belief that a shared devotion to landscape could be enough to break down the ideological walls that keep us tethered to an economic sorting that harms the land and us. Still, making environmental conservation a major plank of your candidacy for the Pennsylvania House of Representatives in a rural district is risky. Or maybe it's just a bad idea if winning is a goal.

Nevertheless, in the overly nerdy manner of an overly nerdy person, I spoke frequently about Article I, Section 27 of the Pennsylvania Constitution: "The people have a right to clean air, pure water, and to the preservation of the natural, scenic, historic and esthetic values of the environment."

I was first introduced to that clause in Sandra Steingraber's essay, "The Fracking of Rachel Carson." The piece offers a remarkable confluence of my sense of Pennsylvania, and I credit it with stoking some of the ecopolitical fire that spurred my campaign. Fracking, of course, has been at the center of political debate in gas-rich Pennsylvania for quite awhile now, the latest destructive innovation deployed to extract wealth at the expense of people who live on the land that has it. Alongside that usual critique, Steingraber also writes in the essay about Carson's eventual cancer, something Steingraber suggests was likely caused by environmental contamination. That irony is also one of the sad, shared fates of many who live in postindustrial places.

At risk of revealing too much about my embarrassing political optimism, I saw Article I, Section 27 as an inviolable, rational way to appeal to conservative voters suspicious of candidates devoted to environmental conservation. Republicans I mean, of course. They love the Constitution, right? And amendments in particular? Isn't that what we hear all the time? The constitutional excerpt seems like a slam dunk.

Yes. Yes. I know.

Aldo Leopold was absolutely prescient about the underlying obstacle to conservation, a concept in full view at the Farm Bureau's Legislative Tour. "We abuse land because we see it as a commodity belonging to us," he writes. "One basic weakness in a conservation system based wholly on economic motives is that most members of the land community have no economic value."

Still, I hold onto Steingraber, and Carson, and Leopold, and the nature of how we might define a "land community." Among the more dire effects of industrial philosophy is the way relationships of land and commodity are fashioned. First of all, a person is viewed as separate from the land. Then the land is defined by what economic value it can produce. Finally, a person is reattached to the land where they live, this time with that new sense of economy intact, so the person becomes a commodified resident of a commodified locale. More simply, if you happen to live where, say, fracking land can produce wealth, then you exist to be fracked. At the risk of further naivete, I contend that helping people understand that would do much to change the politics of America.

* * *

Maybe this should be obvious: Places like Crawford County aren't inclined to like political candidates who define themselves as conservationists. It's the kind of place that favors candidates who thump the Bible and cherrypick references to the Constitution. They don't thump Article I, Section 27. They don't thump any of the parts of the Bible that can be read as yoking environmental stewardship to faithfulness.

My hometown was long marked by coal. In recent years, it's been claimed by gas, the feverish speculation of a Marcellus Shale boom that never quite materialized. That blind hope struck Crawford County, also. In 2014, local officials wrote an entire strategic economic recovery plan that pinned our future on expansions in the fracking industry. The report includes images of the crumbling buildings that demonstrate the legacy of abandonment, and it acknowledges the problems the county faces with decaying housing stock, and aging infrastructure, and a general lack of cash. It even references how the history of the county is yoked to the first site of the American oil industry, Titusville, which boomed then went bust, the inevitable cycle of the fossil fuel industry. The report fails to anticipate the specter of any potential bust in fracking.

This is the larger political point. The deterioration of the region has never been worth improving, not politically. Progress can only ever be described within the language of industry. And we keep betting on the same old failures. *Think of the jobs*, folks say. They don't tally losses, or recurring bad faith "investment," to the evident scars of deterioration and desperation that abound. Many of our communities were built on the hopes of an industry that long ago figured out that bankruptcy and hopping town work well for preserving shareholder wealth.

The scars of my childhood landscape make that clear. Look through the woods, and you'll still find giant black slag heaps abandoned by companies during the early days of strip mining before the law recognized that open, toxic waste dumps were bad. Nothing grows on the heaps, the surface temperature too hot in the summer sun to allow seeds to germinate. You can find unreclaimed gouges, too, the old shelves of land where heavy equipment scraped its way through the earth to expose the coal seams. In places like this, a substance called yellow boy—iron hydroxide—grows in roadside seeps. You can't hide the damage. Twolick Creek, which shaped the valley where the farm lies, ran red my entire childhood, the rocks covered in rust from the iron sulfide leeching out of the mines underneath.

The tainted creek has gotten better, at least. Reclamation wetlands were built to filter the water with natural grasses and reeds. There's even a county park a short walk from my parents' farm, with a trail around the catchment pond, the industrial reclamation project turned into a multiuse recreation project. It isn't exactly beautiful, but it's better than the black slag pile that used to be there, where kids from town smoked dope, smashed beer bottles, and pissed in the red-running creek.

Beneath the farm—and by this I mean *way* beneath the farm—a network of deep coal mines crisscross. Those mines have long since closed, along with most of the mines in Pennsylvania coal country. The tunnels remain, and while the law has long required pillars of stable rock to be left beneath houses in mining country, really who's going to check? Subsidence insurance is a thing in coal country, which is to say people buy insurance for the day when their house starts slowly sinking into the collapsing deep mine below. Cracked foundations are one of the legacies of coal, just as the threat of mercury poisoning is a legacy of the still-burning generating stations, just as red- and yellow-stained creek rocks are a legacy of the relentless seepage of mine acid into the watershed. Cracked foundations are the unrecognized legacy of our nostalgia, too. We want to think of the past as a certain way, want to remember ourselves as mighty. It hurts a little too much to admit that we've never mattered as much to others as we do to ourselves.

I was born in a landscape ceded to the interests of coal, and I live as an adult in a landscape always ready to believe the barker's promise of a revitalized fossil fuel energy sector. In the 2019–2020 session, the PA Legislature handed literally billions of dollars in tax breaks to petrochemical projects through overwhelming bipartisan support. Politicians in Indiana County have said the quiet part out loud. They know the county's three coal-fired generating stations are running out of days, but they want them all because there aren't any other jobs.

*   *   *

The family farm used to be covered in corn, hay, and oats. A dairy farmer leased the land on the cheap, a deal that included a share of the feed and some rent. Our animals grew on the feed, and the farmer often failed to pay the rent, which my father usually forgave since farming is hard. Every summer, our pond sludged over in dank algae, fueled by the fertilizers sprayed into the crops. My father complained about this, to no avail. The farmer repeatedly agreed to stop with the heavy fertilizer use, but the farm pond served as annual evidence that his words were built on convenience. His words were, in a sense, *political*.

Once my parents retired, they stopped raising sheep and goats, sold their horses, and put the remaining chickens in the freezer. They decided to change their relationship to the farm as well. They took it out of cultivation and, instead, planted prairie grasses as part of a state soil conservation program. Now, the fields bloom in wildflowers each summer. The old pastures have grown into immature forest, and the farm has ceased to be productive, in the sense we normally use. It has left the ag-industrial economy and rejoined its ecological community. The farm now produces food for pollinators, and cover for wild animals. My father saw a mink last year, for the first time he can remember.

That's the contrast of choice we face as western Pennsylvanians. What we can be versus what we always have been told to be. We have surface damage that will take a long time to heal: tainted water, slag piles, strip mine cuts, and now Trump flags. On the farm, the giant green brine tanks cannot be removed, and the wells beneath will siphon gas until its run dry. But prairie grasses are tall, and they offer glorious visual contrast, fine towering grasses obscuring the tanks. This is a declaration of desire and hope.

Healing takes time, the deep healing, the healing of our values. That's our choice, even if it's a hard one. We can choose to look at those grasses, or we can choose to look at the horizon, the generating station, the long industrial demand of productivity. What are we, as Appalachians, as the industrial belt rusted over by abandonment if we aren't productive?

We can plant different seeds, but only if we have the patience to let them germinate. This is partly a specific call to environmental conservation, for rural Pennsylvanians to stop accepting that *exploitation* is all our land is—and all we are—good for. Recovery is possible if we just decide we want to opt out of what has been handed to us.

What's in the soil and what we do to the soil is what's in us and what we do to ourselves. Coal, gas and wells, and false hopes and fissured hatreds that have been sown, what we allowed to be sown, what we sow ourselves, acting surprised when disastrous flowers of decaying housing stock, opioid abuse, and job loss spring from our vacant lots. This is the curse we allow when we either vote badly or blame others for voting badly, when we refuse to engage the reality of rural despair.

This might be a small act, but it is an important one, a gesture of faith in the future and commitment to recovery. Politicians rarely look to the wisdom of rejuvenation. It doesn't win votes. In turn, we don't look at wild grasses and think about how planting different seeds leads to different futures.

At home, on the farm, where I once wandered as a kid through endless rows of uniform corn, I now watch coreopsis blow in the wind. Fields that used to open in deep annual furrows are now secured by deeper perennial root mats. There are no more spraying tractors misting the fields. The pastures have started to disappear in stands of new forest. In autumn, the prairie grasses brown and dry, and stay, Frost be damned here, the gold perpetual.

This is what I have come to love most about the farm now, as an adult who lives too far away or maybe not far enough, when I can return in November and walk a warm day among blowing grasses backlit by sun, low light, stems concealing the horizon if I crouch. I walk the gas well roads when I roam the farm. I am aware of that irony. They make it easier to travel. But I relish the middle finger of the farm, a high spot in the county that refuses both strip mine gouging and tractor-flipping farming. Instead, my parents demanded the land become itself, turn away from what it has been told to be, has been forced to be.

* * *

Contradictions abound. Selling giant bales of plastic-wrapped switchgrass is among the most profitable portions of the seed company's business these days. The switchgrass is highly absorbent, and it turns out to be an excellent product to contain gas and oil spills at drilling sites. That means that the fortunes of the company are tied directly to the fracking of Pennsylvania.

"Restoration" is a slippery word. I like to hear it within the context of restoring landscapes, in the way the seed owner described to me the wisdom of native grasses, and soil security, and how the turf-busting colonial agriculture that "settled" large swaths of the United States wrecked the balance of the continent's natural grassy ecosystem. I like to hear "restoration" in the way I heard him enthusiastically explain how fields of switchgrass can help filter tainted runoff before it makes its way into the Chesapeake Bay.

But "restoration" is also useful in describing cleanup, and legally mandated environmental laws that force companies to comply with baseline restrictions for land conservation. Restoration, in this context, isn't necessary romantic or even ecological. It's simply a cost of business or, for the seed company, a market for switchgrass. I see an uncomfortable moral ambiguity here, when a company can be both thrilled at the prospects for selling aster seed to create ground cover underneath solar fields and the dollars to be made helping drillers frack the shit out of our state.

It's probably less ambiguous than I want it to be. It's just economic. Restoration and conservation are both defined in relationship to the understructure of industrial concept, not as the means for recovery but instead as a way to make money within the system that exists.

This particular seed company, in fact, got its start growing crown vetch, a noxious invasive plant that blooms pretty much everywhere now. Decades ago, road engineers needed a way to prevent erosion from soil exposed by road construction. Crown vetch presented itself as an ideal product: cheap, fast-spreading, able to secure a hillside rapidly. So various states started planting it on roadsides, and the seed company defined a market for itself.

Jen and I battle crown vetch in our front yard gardens. It seems to appear overnight, and it acts in the way of noxious invasive, choking out every other plant on its way to domination. We hate vetch, particularly because we tore out most of our front lawn years ago, replacing it with native wildflowers and tall grasses, and the vetch works overtime to choke it out. Our wildflower effort has been a tremendous success, from our perspective. Every summer, our yard blooms with a cyclical shift of wildflowers, from early season yellows, to whites, to the final flourishes of purple asters late in autumn. Bees and hummingbirds and butterflies abound, even within our relatively small wild space in the middle of town.

Vetch doesn't care about such diversity. It believes in the economy of self. Or, rather, vetch has no belief at all, just grows, just is what it is. Vetch strikes me as the ideal metaphor for Aldo Leopold's sense of land community. Vetch thrives now because misguided people decided it had *value*, measured in dollars, even though it degraded the value of the ecosystem. The nature of its invasive, choking existence is not an error. It is, in fact, precisely why it was valuable. Vetch also seems like an apt political analogy.

* * *

In 2014, the tiny municipality of Grant Township, in my home Indiana County, decided to go to political war with the fracking industry. To frack a well, you have to pump large quantities of water. That's how you crack the rock, through the force of relentless pressure. This water, however, isn't water exactly. Instead, it's fracking fluid, a slurry containing various compounds that make it work. You can't know what's in the fluid, though, because frackers have gained legal protections for the "trade secrets" of their blends. Suffice it to say, you wouldn't want to drink it.

The fracking water doesn't stay in the fracked well, though. It's sucked back out into tanker trucks and discarded elsewhere. Sometimes, less scrupulous drillers just spray it out of the back of their trucks onto dirt roads. That's generally illegal though so-called brine water from conventional oil wells is still sometimes used as "dust control" on rural roads. In Pennsylvania, that practice was banned in 2018, but the GOP-controlled legislature would like to make it legal again, effectively turning the entire network of rural dirt roads into open-air waste sites. Brine water isn't good for waterways, as you might guess.

But the wastewater from fracking can't, at the moment, be legally discarded that way. Partly because we know it carries low levels of radioactivity, but mostly because, even though we don't know the mixture's components, we know it isn't particularly healthy. One of the preferred methods of wastewater disposal is to squirt it into "injection wells." In Ohio, that has caused small earthquakes.

No one really knows for sure whether or not the fluid will stay in the injection wells. The fracking industry says it will. They also say fracking poses no risks to groundwater despite clear evidence that it has tainted nearby wells. And in places like Indiana County, we'd be wise to wonder about the rigidity of our rock. There are so many miles of abandoned underground coal mines that you're almost always over or nearby an old mine, which itself might have become flooded by groundwater that becomes poisoned with sulfur and ferrous oxide. Driving back roads in places like Indiana County, you'll find the places where rainbow-slicked water seeps into streams, or yellow sulfur cakes on a trickle of water leaking out of a mine, or the creek still bleeds rusty red.

Grant Township was supposed to get an injection well, and Grant Township said no. They passed an ordinance against it, and they were sued by the Pennsylvania Department of Environmental Protection, likely at the behest of the drilling industry or those who champion it. Grant Township voted to reconfigure its municipal organization, becoming a "Home Rule" jurisdiction to give itself more control over governance. But the state still refused their right to block the well. And the fight continues in the courts because the Department of Environmental Protection argues they alone have the legal right to award or deny permits for injection wells.

I know Grant Township well. Back in the days, I worked as a reporter for the *Indiana Gazette* and Grant was among the many small, rural townships I covered. It's the kind of place where the elected township supervisors are often also the township road crew since much of the governmental work is about maintaining the dirt and gravel roads and bridges, and plowing snow. When I went to township meetings in places like Grant Township, they were usually held within view of the old dump trucks used to keep everything running. A lot of the business addressed the price of road stone and fuel.

In *Local Elections and Politics of Small Scale Democracy*, Eric Oliver, Shang Ha, and Zachary Callen address the space of the truly local in politics. In races for city council, or mayor, or county commissioner, voters make decisions about direct concerns. Roads, bridges, school taxes. The consequences of these elections are immediately impactful, and the behavior of voters in these elections might be considered as the most rational we see. Issues are issues, lived and experienced, and the branding of national concepts of party matter a lot less than they do in federal elections, or should.

Parties still dominate, of course. Local politicians inhabit parties proportionate to the partisan share of their jurisdictions. Crawford County, for example, has been voting steadily for Republicans since the beginning of the Republicans, and Crawford County has a local government dominated by Republicans. Our Board of Commissioners is pretty much always two Republicans and one Democrat, and that's only because the law stipulates that all three can't be from the same party.

I think about the rural township meeting rooms a lot these days. I think about the smell of engine oil and grease, the suspicion the supervisors first cast my way when I called them about visiting the meetings. No reporter had ever done that before. They were used to doing business quietly, not in an untoward way, but without attention. This was in the late 1990s, and already the conservative lean of rural places made for suspicion of "the media." That meant I often heard supervisors utter the words "off the record" frequently if only before saying something completely benign and unobjectionable about road mainte- nance. The opposition between Republicans and Democrats hadn't yet collapsed into its present disaster. You could chuckle about the divisions, and roll your eyes at a codger's suspicion at a reporter showing up at a public meeting.

I think, now, that the definition of "native" versus "invasive" was in play. It's remarkable how quickly the shift from local to interloper happens. Five minutes down the road, and you can become a foreigner. Such distinctions aren't necessarily geographical, I think. Instead, they are conceptual, delineated through class, profession, and relative wealth. I grew up in a town of 15,000 and live now in a town of 12,000. In the surrounding counties, each of those small towns is defined as "the city." The big place, with all of the implications of rural versus urban divides. At the same time, the towns are clearly "rural" if you're living in Pittsburgh, which is itself the boondocks if you're living in New York or LA.

When I think back to my days covering township news in municipal garages, I think about these distinctions, and I think about how we'd all do well to consider the moments we delineate between local and invasive, when we are derisive and disdainful, when we fail to recognize the integrity of a place relates directly to how the place functions.

In township garages, politics carried visceral clarity. The nearby dump truck made it clear, as did the fact that the people running the government also ran the road grader. I remember one of these meetings—it might have been Grant Township, though I can't recall—when the supervisors were complaining about people "from the city" buying farmhouses on dirt roads, then complaining about the dust. The newcomers wanted the township to pave the dirt roads.

But it would make no sense, the supervisor said. It would cost too much, bankrupt the budget. He shook his head. How could you buy a house on a dirt road and be surprised by dust?

His point is clear, grounded in the practical, and it serves as a terrific analogy for the way daily measures of governance are experienced differently by the swaths of people we overgeneralize as rural and urban. The township supervisor's scorn was not ideological though I imagine today it likely would be. Or, at the very least, pundits would leverage the story to deliver their own ideological preference.

Worst of all, political strategists have figured out how to leverage the practicalities of "parochial" concerns into the inferno of cultural battle. As a candidate, paying attention to the deep forest of state-level legislation and community-level struggle, I recognized how often the problems of rural and inner-urban Pennsylvania reflect one another. Poverty. Personal violence. Lack of meaningful employment. Cash-strapped education. In a rational world, the state representatives of Wilkinsburg, Pennsylvania and Guys Mills, Pennsylvania would be on the same side of nearly every issue. They are not. That's clear enough. And it isn't hard to figure out why because racism is also a politically useful campaign tool.

I'll draw it back to fracking, to Grant Township and Braddock, Pennsylvania. Democratic state representative Summer Lee, a progressive Black woman, sought to establish laws that would allow communities to decide for themselves if they want to ban fracking. She knows, and lives, the reality that in America non-white communities are much more likely to suffer the negative consequences of environmental devastation than wealthy, suburban white ones. For this position, and others, Lee wound up having to contend with constant primary challengers supported by the Allegheny County Democratic Party from "moderate" Democrats who won't run afoul of the state's fetishized love of dirty industries. Lee keeps winning elections, though, including in 2022, when she ascended to the US House of Representatives despite intraparty opposition.

Summer Lee and Grant Township ought to be allies. They are not. You will be unsurprised to learn that in 2020, when Donald Trump made a big deal in Pennsylvania about being pro-fracking, running ads about how Joe Biden would threaten the state's economy by banning it, 89 percent of Grant Township voters pulled the lever for Trump.

The "parochial" concerns of local politics have been utterly consumed by the open symbolism of grievance. Confederate battle flags. "Let's Go Brandon." Racist dog whistling. AR-15 silhouettes as personal iconography. The usual symbols of the political landscape of the Trumpian years, all of it concealing the reality of our shared abandonment.

*   *   *

We've been harmed by the invasive nature of politics. I'll push the metaphor: We set ourselves up for toxic algae blooms, for scumming over, for fetid stenches and putrefaction. Vetch creeps over us while we sleep, threatening to choke us. Maybe this isn't as figurative as I want it to be. Cancer clusters. Generational violence. Low wages. Poverty. Joblessness and the working poor. Dollar stores and Walmarts and decaying downtowns. Opioids. Despair.

Strategically, without a doubt, it was ridiculous for me to think that an environmentally conscious platform would appeal in my rural district. The force of social propaganda has been too strong, the specter of the Green New Deal spit from between gritted teeth because it makes for easy political shorthand. Even though the Green New Deal—not even a *thing*, just a gathering of intentions—is built on the promise within an industrial evolution focused on jobs that sustain our land and ourselves. The moronic simplicity of campaign culture shortens it to an attack on rural working people.

Just give us those last ten years of the dirty coal plant, the GOP says in my hometown. Just give us another decade of dwindling jobs in the mines. Just let us poison our water so drilling companies can get rich and leave town. Just don't look at Titusville and Youngstown and Erie and all of the many places in middle America that experienced the bust of having their fortunes tied to the whims of industrial exploitation. Dirty air and water are just the price we have to pay, pretty much forever.

The Pennsylvania legislature has granted, in a strongly bipartisan manner, billions of dollars of tax abatements to subsidize the development of a petrochemical "cracker" plant in the Ohio Valley and to generally support the market for fracked natural gas. Bipartisan. So many Democrats happy to toss public dollars at a project that will bring gobs of profit for multinational energy companies and, in the case of the cracker plant, supply only 800 permanent jobs.

We have to read such politics as threats, as ideological extortion. We have to understand that no one cares about rural Americans, not really, not politically. Politics demands that we accept violence and harm as our cost of living.

I understand the economics. I understand that most rural places have no other choices, not good ones. We've been reliant on dirty industry for so long, and we have experienced pain for so long, we'll do anything to avoid more pain. But fossil energy has been dying my entire life, with persistent calls for decades demanding the development of what we now call a "just transition." Or "energy independence," which has just become a euphemism for drill, baby, drill.

Industry has never cared about the harm they inflict on rural America. Politicians still say, out loud, that they're fine killing our chances for a sustainable economy, that they're fine killing people. Around here, we keep voting for that, which is just another way to prop up our own abuse at the hands of ourselves.

That's Appalachia. That's the Rust Belt. That's the Pennsylvania GOP spinning their bullshit nothings about economy and fiscal conservatism. That's American politics.

Rural America is an experimental zone where politicians seed new strains of noxious ideological weeds. It's easy, and accurate, to point out how the GOP has been the primary purveyor of that experiment in state houses across the country. It's harder, but also accurate, to recognize that the Democratic Party has also treated rural America like an abandoned lot. The weeds don't matter to national Democrats, because they have decided to accept the fate projected on election night. There's a reason Democrats don't put up a fight in rural America, and the reason is Democratic strategy.

*   *   *

After our tour of the seed company's fields, we gathered around a large box of tables to settle in for the presentations. Members of the Crawford County Farm Bureau executive board laid out their priorities. This was the real point of the day, asking legislators to do something about the issues farmers face. One by one, the speakers offered meticulous, informed commentary on what the farmers of the county needed. Low milk prices were a concern, as they have been for some time. They'd appreciate more legislative price support.

The problems of deficient or nonexistent rural broadband got extended attention. Our kids struggled with doing online school, the farmers said. We need broadband to access markets for our crops, they said. We need it for web-linked farm equipment. If we had broadband, our grown children could stay on the farm or move home, could telecommute and keep the family farm going at the same time. Several mentioned they had no internet access at all, or they could get only pricey satellite "broadband," which is both very expensive and slow.

If you'd walked into that room, unaware of where we were and who was talking, you'd think you'd wandered into a lefty gathering. These were progressive talking points, all of them. The farmers were referencing hard work, and they were asking for governmental assistance to give them the safety net they need. I think one of the members of the executive board literally used the term "safety net," without irony. They were asking for help.

The gathered politicians, Republicans, responded with different versions of, *nope*. They pretended they were working on it, characterized best by their pride in new bills that would allow telecom companies to run internet cables on existing electric poles without renegotiating rights-of-way contracts. This is the best answer they had, which boiled down to protecting the profits of companies. There was no talk of actually investing public money in expanding the utility of broadband, or considering ways to ensure that rural people could afford it if it ever happened to be installed.

I hope the farmers were pissed off by the politicians' dismissive comments, but I'm sure I know how they voted the following month. Not for me. Not for Joe Biden. We know our lives are diminished by the exploitative presence of extractive industry, but in rural America we're also the loudest defenders of our own exploitation.

I left before lunch was served, defeated. Despite the common purpose of those in the room and my political aspirations, I knew there was no point in sticking around. No minds would be moved. There's a metaphor here, as well, about seeds and time and patience.

Outside, the wild grasses blew in the late summer wind. This means nothing politically, but I choose to see it as an expression of faith, There is wisdom in rejuvenation. There is hope in wild grasses. There is potential in planting different seeds to cultivate different futures.

NINE

THIS IS WHY WE LOSE

Meadville's Italian Civic Club is a monolithic windowless building in a downtown Rust Belt block that wears its abandonment clearly. Several nearby rooflines show fine old design, dormers, mansards and well-crafted brickwork marking a long-gone prosperity now covered in cheap vinyl facades. There's a budget wireless service store and a used appliance store. There's a thrift store next door to the Civic Club and a dollar store kitty corner from it. The old Eagles Club aerie across the street was bought by a big box evangelical church that had previously held services at the local movie theater. The Civic Club is across the street from Meadville's Downtown Mall, which gathers together the dollar store, a military surplus store, a secondhand clothing store, a liquor store, a Big Lots!, a diner, the bus station, and the office of the incumbent state representative who has done nothing to alleviate the decline and suffering all around.

You can't walk into the Italian Civic Club and wonder whether or not Meadville needs help. The evidence is all around you, a blaring trumpet call about the consequences of its political abandonment. The region has been plagued by governance concepts of deprivation for at least a generation. The story is familiar, usually pegged to the industrial departures of the latter parts of the twentieth century, when the term "Rust Belt" was coined by Walter Mondale. Reality, as we know, is more complicated, the deprivations having started even before that. On the other side of Crawford County, the small city of Titusville—which fares even worse these days—collapsed in the late nineteenth century when the world's first commercial oil boom collapsed. Lessons have not been learned.

Part of the contemporary political landscape, of course, is how places like this have been tethering themselves to the mysteries of Reaganomics as its potential savior even though the trickle of prosperity promised forty years ago has never arrived. Still, the austerity of Republican economic "conservatism" has aligned with quasi-Libertarian brutishness and steroid-pumped theocratic desire to create the dank conditions of Trumpian kleptocracy as the expressed will of the people. The decayed neighborhood around the Italian Civic Club is the legacy of corporatized politics, where profit is the only measure of importance.

That's the landscape of the Italian Civic Club, where two and a half years ago, his bald head nearly brushing the door frame, wearing his trademark Carhartt puffer jacket and baseline scowl, in walked then Lieutenant Governor John Fetterman. He arrived as one of the chief flacks for the Democratic Party, tasked in 2020 with stirring up voting fervor. That was the point of his visit to Meadville, showing up at the Crawford County Democratic Committee's spring breakfast to inspire action that could lead to electoral wins.

Such events are a combo of political rally and party fundraiser. The party faithful fork over twenty-five bucks for a buffet of the usual spread. Rubbery pancakes. Dripping bacon. Scrambled eggs. Weak coffee. There's an eclectic silent auction of random gift baskets, gift certificates to local businesses, and a hand-hewn tape carpentered by one of the party regulars. In the room, Democrats sit at circular banquet tables. Most are insiders of some kind, both politically and civically. The vibe of the room is similar to that of a Rotary Club gathering, the same regular hobnobbers hobnobbing with the same regulars as always. However, since this is a Democratic gathering in a Republican zone, most of the usual movers and shakers are elsewhere.

I was at the breakfast, too, as a candidate, ostensibly to introduce myself and gather more support. It was February, the primary still to come, but as the only state-level candidate on the ballot I was effectively the nominee and more or less kicking off the public phase of the general election. In theory, the breakfast was the place to tap into the kind of enthusiasm necessary for a hard election. There were contribution checks, too, palmed off to me in ways that felt vaguely dirty even though they would be reported officially on state campaign finance forms.

In 2020, the state Democratic Party was talking about a Blue Wave, much like previous years but this time with an official slogan. But in 2020 there seemed to be a fresh recognition that investments in state legislative elections mattered. On the one hand, voting maps would be redrawn after the 2020 census. In 2010, Republicans had used their majority to carve out extensive gerrymandering across the state, and while their initial maps were ruled unconstitutional by the state Supreme Court, even the court's redrawn maps still heavily favored Republicans. A Democratic majority in 2020 would be a chance to correct that.

On the other hand, and more broadly, the PA Dems seemed to be acknowledging how the GOP had a much stronger state-level strategy, which is to say the GOP actually had a state-level strategy. The result has been unbreakable GOP majorities in "purple" states like Pennsylvania and Ohio. In Pennsylvania, for example, Democrats outnumber Republicans by several percentage points, but the GOP has held majorities in the state legislature for thirty years.

None of us quite understood in February how the rest of 2020 would play out. Covid shutdowns were still a month away, as was the GOP's strategic play of Covid-denial. We were nine months away from the state legislature's GOP majority pretending Joe Biden's election was fraudulent even though their own victories were totally fine, and almost a year from the resultant cockroach insurrection of January 6. I'd like to think, perhaps, the abandonment of the Blue Wave was an emergency strategic response to those events. But it wasn't.

John Fetterman told us that in February of 2020, when the Crawford County Chair handed him the microphone, and everyone applauded, and we were all excited that the state's charismatic giant, shorts-wearing, now-Senator had arrived to drum up some excitement for our own important races. I mean, that's what I thought at first, how cool it was that I might borrow a little energy from his visit, that he had even bothered to come and stump for my downballot race.

"Republicans are ruining the country," he said.

The crowd cheered.

"It's hard being a Democrat here," he said, meaning Crawford County, meaning rural places across the state.

The crowd nodded.

"You know you're going to get walloped," he said.

Wait, what?

"But your job," he said, "is to get out and vote for Joe Biden, because every vote counts."

Wait. Wait. What!?

Applause. The party faithful were thrilled. A political celebrity in our midst! Who had the guts to blister Donald Trump! Like we all do every single day!

Rhetorically, this would have been an excellent moment for Fetterman to reference downballot races, like mine or the one for US House, where an Erie teacher was running to beat a deeply entrenched Tea Party car salesman. Trying to break the GOP hold on these seats would be difficult, he could have said, but it's worth trying. And here are the people trying to do something about that, despite the odds. Let me introduce your next representatives, blah blah blah.

But Fetterman did not say that.

He intoned the year's slogan a few more times. "Back to Blue. Back to Blue. Back to Blue." He said he'd just bought the county party a new computer to replace its shitty old one. The cheered. The Chair beamed.

"Back to Blue. Back to Blue!"

And that was it.

The speech ended with no reference to me or to the US House candidate, nor even to the existence of our races. In fact, Fetterman never even said hello, at least not to me. Then he was out the door, too busy for a prospective state rep's speech. The energy in the room shifted or, perhaps, clarified. By the time I took the microphone, I knew I was just a warm-up act for the headliner, who had already left.

* * *

Two years have passed since my candidacy. I just got home from the polling station, where the incumbent I failed to unseat is running again in a theoretically contested race. It isn't even lunch time, and I know he will win again even though he has barely campaigned. The Democratic challenger has failed to mount a substantive challenge because the siren song of moderation has encouraged a theme of high-road politeness instead of direct attacks at the incivilities of the officeholder. That would seem sensible as the incumbent's social media image is that of a bully. He offers a steady stream of Facebook trolling, where he stirs up outrage and anger, casts aspersions, winks at racism and bigotry, and generally fans the flames of partisan fires he sets. When you see such things, it's easy to get sucked into the illusion that respectability will break party faithfulness. Voters claim they prefer polite discourse, as well, even if voting patterns don't offer any evidence.

The reality is that the incumbent enjoys a registration advantage of close to 40 percentage points in newly redrawn PA House maps, and most people aren't paying attention to his Facebook page. Instead, it's just the den of the faithful, who growl with exactly the kind of voices you hear in fevered national attention. Trump cultists, essentially, who pretend they believe in the Republican Party, but who would, without question, call Abraham Lincoln a RINO if he happened upon today's scene.

The bigger, more frustrating reality is that so many voters pay so little attention to candidates, particularly so-called downballot ones like state representatives. At best, most watch national news coverage that reinforces their partisan beliefs. Lately, as we all know, that has led Republicans to tune into the distorted reality of FOX News and worse, all of which serves to solidify the false stability of partisan identity. When you're running as a downballot candidate, few outside the politically engaged pay attention, partly because they have no way to pay attention. There's precious little local news coverage, and local newspapers in rural areas, if they exist at all, are so beholden to the revenue of local car dealerships that their political coverage craters in the fantasy land of objective evenhandedness. In turn, political coverage willfully ignores elected officials' attempts to, say, pass state legislation overturning the results of the 2020 Presidential election due to imaginary voter fraud that, miraculously, did not apply to their own race.

How, really, do you run a campaign in that atmosphere? As a Democrat, you know two-thirds of local voters are predisposed to distrust or even hate you. At the same time, most voters claim they hate the negative tone of politics. Yet few voters have enough interest to stick with you if you try to explain the nuances of policy on, say, how single-payer healthcare would be a game-changer for the economic prosperity of rural America. That just makes you a Socialist.

After all, the 2022 candidate saw me lose a race trying to do such things, so there's a seeming logic in steering clear of third rails. But that leaves a nearly absolute vacuum of substance in a candidacy, and I have to confess disappointment and annoyance with polite tactics in impolite arenas. All you have as a rural Democrat is the opportunity to make noise. This is hard to accept because you also want to believe you can actually win. But you can't. So you need to make noise.

As much as it hurts to admit this, John Fetterman was exactly right back at the spring breakfast. Strategically, I mean. Within the context of the Democratic Party, I mean. When Fetterman said rural Democrats exist only to minimize the margin of victory for Republicans, that is totally true.

And that is exactly the problem. It's what makes me the angriest about rural politics. I know what the GOP stands for. They've made it plain. But the Democratic Party, as a strategic entity with a single-minded goal of winning elections, offers a coercively Faustian bargain for rural Democrats. Vote for the party, they say, even though the party sees you as cannon fodder. I suppose I have to give Fetterman credit for saying that out loud, perhaps accidentally.

Accelerating my narrative time frame here, from the present tense of yesterday to the future tense of today, Fetterman's strategy will work. He will win his 2022 race for Senate, narrowly, through the execution of an "Every County, Every Vote" strategy. He will receive praise for this, because *strategically* he will run ahead of Joe Biden in some rural areas by a few percentage points, which is enough to win the state of Pennsylvania. But that also means he will pull in only 30 percent of the vote in Crawford County. That's a shellacking, and it's also the same shellacking Joe Biden received in Crawford County. Such margins reflect the utter electoral irrelevance of the Democratic Party in Crawford County: sacrificial voters at the service of candidates who visit only when they want to stump for their own statewide elections.

Strategy is a terrible way to live. Strategy means you think it's a success to pull in a 30 percent share of the vote instead of 28 percent. Strategy means you call it a success when more than two-thirds of county voters go for a celebrity doctor over Fetterman, or when you think it's a good sign that "only" 60 percent of county voters supported the explicitly white Christian nationalist gubernatorial candidate, Doug Mastriano, on the same ticket. Strategy means you think it's worth running for state office by racing toward the tepid middle, or that your job as a downballot candidate it to serve as a rah-rah cheerleader for the party instead of speaking about things that matter in ways that matter.

I mean, if you're going to lose, why not go down in flames? We know elections are more or less confirmation of the sophisticated drawing of district lines, outcomes hewing to registration percentages, with the lines themselves drawn by politicians to establish as few competitive electoral zones as possible. If you're going to run, why not thump some tables, or flip some over, and generally refuse to accept the position of the politely abandoned?

* * *

Our plight as rural Democratic voters is irrelevance. You know that. You see it on every election news piece, where the maps are washed in red, and the pundits wonder how a Democrat could appeal to "rural voters" and explain why extremist right wingers appeal to those same people. There's a lack of nuance in that kind of coverage, of course. No surprise, there.

Politics is a game. It is a ritualized exercise in fashioning party fidelity, grouping chunks of people into stable units of locked-in electoral districts, and governing to secure those geographical divisions and then reinforce the team sport dynamic of political identity.

Games rely on strategy. But strategy is not simply playing by the rules—not when the rules are themselves part of the game. The rules of this game, of elections, are literally manufactured by the parties. In Pennsylvania, you can't even participate in primary elections if you aren't a Democrat or Republican, whether voter or candidate; it's one of a dozen states with closed primaries. Disappointing outcomes for rural Democrats are baked in even if the Democratic Party will never admit it. There's a reason they don't spend money in rural America. Even when they won the fight for an independent redistricting commission to redraw the state legislative maps, the Democratic Party was happy to help the commission create more competitive districts in suburban Pittsburgh and Philadelphia by actually making rural GOP-dominant districts somehow even more reliably red.

This is the cost of business for Democratic strategy. It works, for them, because in 2022 the Democrats actually pulled off a surprising flip of the PA House due to these more competitive suburban districts. They call that a victory, which it is *strategically*. But here, in the boondocks, we're still seen as little other than gun-clinging deplorables living in the flyover wastelands of "Pennsyltucky." As a Democrat living in such a place, you're supposed to be glad about those victories even though nothing has changed, at all, about the prevailing political attitudes of your region.

In *Nine Gates*, Jane Hirshfield writes, "Often, the stories we hold about self and world are subliminal, wielding the power of the unexamined, and thus go unquestioned. But the shaping of art is also a way such hidden narratives are softened, made workable; it brings them into a kind of attention that reaches both conscious and unconscious minds."

We all live inside the stories ingrained by narratives of the collective unexamined. That rural people are conservative. That "conservative" means something. That Democrats will govern in a way that helps the rural. That functional differences between urban and rural struggles exist. Our interests—human interests—are at best a secondary concern to what we deliver on Election Day. We're all disappointed in politicians not because governance is complex, but because strategy is a festering wound of bad-faith decisions oriented in team-sport victories instead of the possibilities of win-win mutual prosperity.

So let's talk about strategy. Let's talk about abandonment. Let's talk about how the strategy of electoral politics means places like Crawford County aren't worth the effort for the Democratic Party. Republicans have been strategic, winning control in state legislatures in even "purple" states like Pennsylvania, largely by coalescing power in red-stained rural zones. But that doesn't happen in a vacuum. Or, rather, it happens because of a vacuum of Democratic investment in rural spaces. That means every race at every level of government, at least where I live, winds up being about culture war issues: guns and abortion and, more than a little, shoring up white nationalism.

"In the beginning of every election cycle, the Democratic Party and all the campaign committees that support candidates look at the raw numbers and put resources into so-called swing states, where the gap between Democratic and Republican registration is less than ten points," Jane Kleeb, the Nebraska Democratic Chair, writes in her *Harvest the Vote*. "Occasionally there will be a bright star candidate that gets the attention of the Democratic Party, but generally, rural candidates are left off the list—a list also given to major donors across the country—of candidates everyone is to invest in for the cycle."

Put another way, the solidly Republican nature of rural areas is a self-fulfilling prophecy. One of the hardest things about being a rural progressive candidate is feeling like you're alone, that knocking on any door means you're probably talking to someone who loathes you, that you're going to overhear tons of casual conversations in hair salons and restaurants about evil Democrats, and you'll have to get your furnace fixed by an asshole who flies a Trump sign in front of his business, who spreads QAnon conspiracy theories online, who will eventually win a seat on a local school board and lead the charge in banning the teaching of Critical Race Theory, even though they don't know what it is beyond a campaign gotcha term. You'll also see your home maligned on national political coverage as a place responsible for the election of these right wingers. And you'll listen to the Democratic Lieutenant Governor—a progressive! A populist! A man of the people!—show up at your political debut and tell everyone your candidacy is pointless.

We're all rural voters, aren't we? In the eyes of the partisans? We are all rural voters because, to political machines, we are all just votes to be tallied. I mean this about you, wherever you live. Politics does not focus on governance. Instead, politics is a myopic fix on maps even when promising a future governance that never quite materializes. I know that sounds jaded enough to be laughable, but it's hard to see it otherwise when nothing changes in your backyard. The local economy still sucks. Local bigots are still elected to the school boards. Local Democrats lose elections, over and over, and then they repeat platitudes about the value of their tepid efforts, about building coalitions for the future or some other bullshit that adds up, essentially, to high water marks of 35 percent moral victory vote tallies. No coalitions are ever built.

* * *

At each of his last two semiannual debates, the incumbent presented an *aw-shucks, I'm just a local dude* argument for his merits. He explained that all he does is go to Harrisburg, think about how most people in Crawford County would vote on each issue, then votes that way too. The perfect representative. Against me, he deployed this in tandem with the suggestion that I was more of a Philadelphia kind of person, a strategically brilliant multi-layered dog whistle.

This is only surface-level practicality, of course, which glosses over the reality that Pennsylvania legislators are paid about $100,000 a year to be full-time professionals. In theory, they should understand the ins and outs of each issue quite a bit more than the average person in their home districts, and then they should vote in ways that help their constituents whether or not it's the obvious direction. Strategically, though, his statement is perfect. The incumbent masks naked political pandering in ostensible evenhandedness, shoring up support for the GOP majority of the district while also saying he absolutely refuses to consider the interests of the non-GOP residents of the region who, even if they happen to be in the minority, measure in the tens of thousands.

What, really, is the point of running in elections like this? As a Democrat, I mean.

* * *

For awhile, I was angry at Fetterman for acting as he did at our spring breakfast, and for saying what he did. But I've come around to the other side. I have come to appreciate the truth of his visit. It would have been fraudulent to suggest that I had a chance. The Democratic machine, of which he has been very much a part despite the aura of his outsider persona, long ago determined that no Democrat has a chance in Crawford County. Again, I say this with less bitterness than you might think. Their strategy is exactly correct.

But it is also very much the strategy of their own design. As rural Democrats, I think we need to see that for what it is. I think the same is true for Democrats from marginalized communities, most of whom receive only surface legislative support in exchange for their votes. I mean, I would argue this is true for pretty much all marginalized Democrats, members of a large club that exists primarily for the benefit of, well, not you. Consider abortion rights, and the way the Supreme Court destroyed them, and how the Democratic Party controlled the House, Senate, and Presidency, and how the decision that would decimate Roe v. Wade was leaked months ahead of time, and how not only did the Democratically controlled government fail to pass a law to codify women's rights to bodily autonomy, it didn't even put a bill up to do so. Worse, Joe Biden used the destruction of Roe v. Wade as a campaigning chip for the midterms, promising to codify abortion law *if* voters secured a majority in the House and Senate. I am aware that it's unlikely the Democratic trifecta indicated enough votes to actually pull off the codifying of such a law. But why do we accept not trying? This is why we are all effectively rural voters whose actual interests matter only, let's say it together, *strategically*.

One of the dark benefits of living in the land of the right wing is getting to see the reality of those Democratic abandonments. It is distinctly true that Democratic politicians are losers here. Yet Democrats or Democratic organizers are doing no work to establish mechanisms to shift values. All they offer, again and again, are vague promises in exchange for our votes. And those vague promises, as Fetterman made clear, are not about helping us but, instead, just that they'll help elect Democrats elsewhere.

Another hard truth we need to accept is that the rural support of Donald Trump actually makes a lot of rational sense. Yes, rational, as in rural Americans know they receive nothing but disdain or lip service from politicians, all of whom work primarily for the interests of not-rural people. So Donald Trump offered at least a way to say, *fuck you*. It's a pretty damned harmful way to say that, of course, and the consequences of the accompanying racism, bigotry, and crony capitalism cannot be ignored. The people who voted for Donald Trump still can't find it within themselves to consider harm inflicted on others. But, yeah, I get it.

What I am really trying to say is that the Democratic Party deserves blame for that, too. What I am really trying to say is that as rural progressives, we have to start refusing the roles in which we are cast. We need to realize that we don't have to accept being the expendable rural wing of a party that hasn't proven it cares about us. We should run candidates knowing that our only leverage might be refusing to go along with what the Democratic Party wants us to do. We know the GOP hates us, but we have to recognize that the Democratic Party treats rural Democrats as political pawns, as numbers on a spreadsheet calculating vote totals.

No more. That's my plea. No more tepid campaigns designed to cater to the illusion of moderation. We need to recognize that it's okay to want more for ourselves than is offered. We can stop accepting that our job is to support top-of-ticket Democrats. Until they show up for us, really show up, maybe we should stop. That might be the only thing that wakes the party up to rural citizens because losing us would mean losing Pennsylvania.

This is where I shall utter the unspeakable: third party. I know third party candidates are irrelevant. But here in rural America, we're irrelevant already. Sometimes, the only way to become relevant is to refuse to play by the rules that designate you as irrelevant. Consider that the revulsion of third party or independent support—blaming Ralph Nader for the 2000 election of George W and Jill Stein for the 2016 election of Trump—is a manufacturing of compliance to party faithfulness. It's Foucault, y'know? Discipline by your peers, which serves the interests of the powerful.

At campaign events, it's easy to see the areas of common interest. Farmers who need reliable broadband. Impoverished neighbors who can't afford rent or food. Woodlands and fields wrecked by extractive industry that makes a mint then leaves. Yet we collapse into the comfortable patterns of partisan fidelity and revulsion. Rural progressives might do better if they start by flipping the bird at the DNC or, at the very least, refuse to be quiet about our abandonment. Getting non-Democrats to listen might require that message to come from outside the Democratic Party. Otherwise, it's just too easy for the GOP to say, *Democrats can't win here*, which is the same thing the Democrats have been saying all along.

* * *

Once Joe Biden became the official nominee, the Pennsylvania Democratic Party folded itself into his official campaign. Even the "Back to Blue" push was sacrificed, the posters and t-shirts tossed, and the official state party staffer emails switched over mainstream to reflect the party's full emphasis on his campaign.

Any talk of flipping the legislature in that crucial year ceased. A local PA Dems staffer had to sneak my name onto the official phone banking scripts, which were written to emphasize Biden and only Biden. I got phone calls from other party staffers, too, inviting me to fold all of my volunteers into their top-of-ticket efforts—not as a way to bolster my campaign but as a way for them to get more work for their guy. They saw my candidacy as belonging to them. I refused.

I'm not sure why I was surprised to discover that Pennsylvania's "Back to Blue" had been just an early marketing slogan, to be replaced with a wholesale co-optation of every Democratic race as a mechanism for national interests in "competitive" districts.

This is what Democratic strategy looks like for rural candidates. Because, at heart, politics is about what you're gonna get and what you have to give, and Fetterman knows that landscape.

He's a senator now because he understands that landscape. And, to be clear, we're better off with him as a senator and, in general, there's no doubt we're better off with Democrats because the current consequence of GOP tendencies is dark, indeed.

But still. That's the bind. Our own irrelevance seems central to the deal, as it has been for so long. Indeed, the strategic brilliance of the GOP has been to recognize the despair of those left behind by the money-mongering of Reaganomics, to cultivate that despair while concealing the cause of it, and to then build a powerful voting bloc across the country.

I don't have much hope that the Democratic Party will wake up to this, largely because I think there's nothing to wake up to. They know what they're doing. They have a strategy, and it involves not investing in the areas where being not-a-Republican means you are always a loser. Politics hates losers.

* * *

After John Fetterman took the microphone and said rural Democrats don't matter beyond what we could do for the party, I wish I had channeled my anger. Now, I see my own campaign as having succumbed to the strategy of tepid messaging, at least in that moment. I was afraid to offend Democrats, so I shied away from publicly criticizing fatalistic Democratic messaging.

I wish I'd dropped the pretense of party solidarity that morning and used my time saying what we're told we're not allowed to say. *Thanks for nothing.* Because until the Democratic party actually offers authentic support to rural areas, rural people, and rural candidates, nothing is all we will get.

Even now, I shudder when I think about the courage I did not have that morning. We all know the tracks we're supposed to stay within. In politics, it's too easy to decide to allow the hard truths to go unspoken because you worry about the votes that might disappear. I wasn't ready, in the moment, to embrace the turmoil of real resistance to the broken system of party politics.

There's always the risk of offense. Say the wrong thing, and suddenly fellow Democrats aren't on your side, and you can't afford to lose any of them. That's what it feels like, at least. And the fear isn't unwarranted, as I have watched many staunch Democrats sneer at their own candidates when the candidates punch back against Republican attack ads, for example.

"Both sides are awful," they say.

A supporter emailed me during my campaign to warn me of a "negative" tone when I criticized the dominant GOP leadership in Harrisburg for how it abdicated public health responsibilities during the early days of Covid. Our political atmosphere is charged by a desire for toxic détente. Way too many Democratic voters are happier with the cruelty of faux bipartisanship than with truth telling.

At the same time, the GOP has figured out that pugnacious aggression works. It fires up the angry parts of their base, and when opponents defend themselves, it turns away "reasonable" Democrats, who prefer the illusion of the high road. The high road is a laudable goal, but it's also a losing strategy when you're getting bulldozed.

I'm ready now to be loud, to say what I wish I had at the breakfast. If you're a rural Democrat, whether progressive or not, you are forced to vote for Democrats who don't care about you. Republicans, in turn, hate you because you are a Democrat. So you're left with a decision between casual disdain and active loathing.

Is this all we want? Is this all we deserve?

Progress isn't about the Democratic Party winning in places like rural Pennsylvania. That just flips the binary. Winning is just storming a different Capitol. That might be hard to accept because it's easy to fall into the trap of thinking that politics somehow matters, and by that I mean the power, and ideology, and polling, and thinking that being a Democrat or a Republican matters in some fundamental way.

To be ignored is to be erased. It doesn't take much deep thinking to get there, but rural America—rural progressives—live in erasure. We have been squashed into a binary nonexistence of either living in protest or not existing at all, and too few people are willing to consider the futures that might include us.

Maybe that's my greatest advice for rural Democrats running in places like Crawford County. We need to speak out about those speculative nonfictions. We need to give up on winning and give up on top-down bullshit strategies. We need to say what needs to be said even when a lot of our ire will be directed at our own alleged allies. We have to refuse to play the game as it is delivered to us because that game is designed so we lose all the time. We have nothing to lose by getting loud about our abandonment, nothing to lose when we refuse to buy into the goals of strategic spreadsheet watchers of the DNC, nothing to lose when we alienate those who have already decided we will lose.

This is why we lose, I should have said at the spring breakfast. *What John Fetterman just said is why we lose. We have learned to be grateful when a prominent Democrat drops in for ten minutes, and that is not enough. We cannot allow that to be enough.*

I know the silence that would have followed. The awkward clink of a fork against a plate. The smell of congealed bacon grease. Slow head shakes from folks who had spent good money to listen to this. The rising anger of the party insiders. The sounds of votes scurrying beneath the floorboards when the lights click on.

Well, I should have done it. I should have gone ahead and lost some votes at the breakfast. Hell, I was going to lose the election anyway even if I hadn't quite admitted that to myself yet. I ran to lose, and that's not a bad thing. I wish I had tried losing harder.

I wish I had shown the Crawford County Democrats what losing can *really* look like. Go down on fire instead of shaking the hands of those who see you only as a tool to be used for their own purposes. Self-immolation as an act of political defiance. That's my earnest plea for rural Democrats, candidates and voters alike. Light it up. Because the losing we've been suffering isn't going to get better until we do.

TEN

SUCCESSION

I grew up in, moved away from, returned to, and lost an election in heavily forested Western Pennsylvania, a state named specifically for the impressiveness of its trees: Penn's Woods. When William Penn gained the charter for the land from Charles II in 1681, more or less all of the colony's twenty-nine million acres would have been dense, old-growth forest. By the end of World War I, heavy timbering had reduced the state's forest coverage to a low of thirteen million acres, which has since recovered to seventeen million acres.

While a walk in these contemporary woods often winds past thick old trees and heavy undergrowth, the vast majority of even old-seeming forests are new growth. The ancient forests of the region long ago succumbed to farm clearing, timbering, and general development. Hardwoods like oak and chestnut were cleared in support of, first, the British economy and, later, a new America. Cleared land turned to pasture, and where farms failed or where abandoned, conifers took to the vacant grasslands. Those, too, were often felled, and the hardwoods grew once more in muddy, stumped clear-cuts, leading to the sort of mixed forest that now covers Pennsylvania and other heavily wooded sections of the Northeast.

Measured on the timeline of European activity in North America, sustained periods of clear-cutting tally in the order of two. But these ancient forests experienced perhaps countless cycles of change over their many years, in a process first named "succession" by French Naturalist Adolphe de la Malle in the eighteenth century. By tracking the way plants repopulated cleared forests, de la Malle recognized the seed of contemporary environmental science, which now recognizes the constant dynamism of natural landscapes. More simply, what I think of as "the woods," say the brambled slashing at the top of my parents' farm or the oak-filled squirrel hunting grounds on another nearby family acreage, is really a product of chance occurrences, organic propagations and, often, recovery from various catastrophic events.

In Pennsylvania, only a handful of actual "old growth" remains, in a few contained patches of forest preserved by the timber companies either in uncommon recognition of the rapid destruction splintering at the axe or, perhaps, in a cagey preservation of high-dollar, tight-grained old wood. Only in places like Hearts Content, not too far from my current home in northwestern Pennsylvania, can a person walk among a reasonable version of the sort of forests that predated human consumption of wood. Here, the forest is marked by more or less homogeneous vegetation as these climax forests, by definition, contain low species diversity. Each member of the community is essentially perfectly suited to the environment at hand.

Defined somewhat imprecisely, inertia describes a universal and undeniable preference for stability. Succession, then, describes the arboreal process of inertia. In the way forests repopulate themselves and build, once again, toward stasis, we see both a remarkable process of renewal and a disconcerting preference for rigidity.

*　*　*

Let me consider the successions of my family:

My mother grew up in Gary, Indiana, the daughter of a Chicago postman and an elementary school secretary. For unclear reasons, but Catholic faith at least among them, my grandmother sent her away to a boarding school in South Bend. At St. Mary's, my mother met the Notre Dame boys, even went to one of their formals with Perry Como's son. After high school, my mother moved to Chicago's St. Xavier College, then into the second-grade classrooms of Kokomo, Indiana, later to Monroe County, where she worked with the students who struggled the most. One of them, sixteen years old and still yet to read, presented my mother with a bag of persimmons from her backyard tree. Suspicious of the pungency of the fruit and the dripping juice seeping through the bag, my mother worried about a connection between the decay of the student's school clothes and general rot. My mother thanked her before secretly tossing the persimmons in the school incinerator. As she turned away from the flames, she saw the girl wave from a passing school bus. My mother has always wondered how much or how little the girl understood about the guilt of that moment, when her own failure to understand the ripeness of persimmons may or may not have meant so much.

My father grew up in an eastern Pennsylvania whistle-stop village. Never prosperous, the family ran the local general store, where he pumped gas and dropped nickels into their bootleg slot machine. His father ran shovel at an open-pit anthracite mine, spent large periods of my father's childhood living away from home during the work week. When anthracite demand plummeted after World War II, his father took odd jobs around town clearing brush or selling chickens or cutting trees. His father boxed under the ring name "Farmer John," earning greasy dollars by exploiting his natural talent for absorbing punches if not the talent for landing them. My father's uncle picked up the trash at nearby Fort Indiantown Gap, locally called "The Gap." His uncle plucked fraying fatigues from the refuse, gave them to my grandmother, who patched the holes and gave them to my father as school clothes. My father ate the persimmons that grew on his grandparents' tree. My father learned fast that his Pennsylvania Dutch accent led only to jeers from students and teachers, who, in this already hard-up part of Pennsylvania, understood the accent as the mark of someone, at least, poorer than themselves.

* * *

Geographical disturbance—an overly fancy way of saying "leaving home"—is the most Appalachian-cliché aspect of my life. Returning, also, is part of that deal. Jen and I started our long arc back to home by leaving for the desert southwest, into a landscape that seemed a photo-negative of Pennsylvania. Dryness for humidity. Scrub desert for mixed hardwoods. Heat for cold.

Just east of our southern Arizona house, earth moving equipment made short work of the desert shortly after we moved in. Thickets of mesquite, ocotillo, cholla and prickly pear were mounded into heaps ready for burning. Plumes of black diesel exhaust scoured giant blades across the earth, exposing red desert. My wife and I lived, then, in Sierra Vista, a small city that grew out of the brothels that used to flank Fort Huachuca, home of the Buffalo Soldiers. Now, the fort serves as a communications and intelligence proving ground for the US Army, and seedy old Fry Town has grown into 40,000-strong Sierra Vista.

As with all desert towns, growth and sprawl are indistinguishable: New homes pop up south and east, cutting away the desert to make way for pseudo-adobe houses. In the former desert just east of our old neighborhood—which itself had been carved out of the shrub around the time of my birth in the 1970s—foundations appeared quickly, sprouting from the earth much like forest mushrooms sprout on rotting logs in the Pennsylvania woods. Crews worked quickly, and frames sprang up, followed by sheathing, followed by stucco. Inside, the plumbers and electricians spun the systems, followed by the sheetrockers, then crews of finish carpenters who tacked on the moldings and trim. Houses appear as if in time lapse films. Crews remove the desert, then head to the next place.

Just beyond this new development, barbed wire demarcated the end of development. Signs declared it property of the local water authority. A dry gulch wound through that part of the landscape, a small chasm of dust and rocks for most of the year. During summer, however, thunderstorms build over the Huachuca Mountains and on most afternoons, hard rain floods the draw. Water runs thick, the ocotillo bloom, and desert drab becomes a truer shade of green. After the rains, frog songs emerge, along with flowers, and life, and all that makes the desert much more than a wasteland.

For a housing development, such action in water proves inconvenient. The draws are converted to culverts. The rushing flow of desert water is diverted into proper channels, redefined as wastewater.

* * *

Our next departure was to France, into a small apartment in a quiet corner of Paris, where language failed me and where the horizon disappeared behind layers of Parisian architecture. I became lost in France, or perhaps finished my journey into lost.

I came to Paris as an obedient child and quiet student who declined the prestigious college where my mother used to dance to enroll in the local one because free tuition was one of my father's professional perks. A communications major becomes a biology major becomes a music major becomes a business major becomes a physics major becomes a music major again becomes an English major. Add an MFA from the city down the road, then write for a newspaper, start teaching for a college, quit for a desert PhD, quit again three months in, earn $500 aggregate as a freelance writer, move to Paris.

I came to Paris also as a twenty-eight-year-old who had always chosen the path of least resistance. My great rebellions in life had been majoring in English and spending a college fund not spent on college to bankroll living in Paris. I wonder, now, twenty years after France, if the terror I then called culture shock was better described as growing up.

At 66 rue d'Alleray, I lived without a target, and targets function for the mind very much as a safety net functions for the man on the wire. Targets imply path, are the destination of properly applied rationality, the clear and undeniable motion toward success. This, in Paris, was what I had given away. I had no particular aim, only nebulous ideas of writing and golf. Neither of these professions offered much hope of independent success, let alone stability. And, as it turned out, my career as a professional golfer amounted to half a dozen last-place finishes and career earnings of minus $5,000.

In the language of ecological succession, "disturbance" is defined as a "temporary change in average environmental conditions." For a forest, disturbances include invasive species, flooding, logging, fire, and windthrow. It is this last term, I think, that describes my early moments of despair in Paris, when I lay in bed at night sobbing for some hard-felt loss, terrified of the days that lay ahead of me. In the forest, windthrow describes the periodic uprooting of trees knocked down by wind, itself a force visible only by its effect: lightly fluttering drapes, or desk papers whisking in a sudden gust, or the cyclonic dust devils of Arizona, or the sheared away tree that glistens wet after a summer thunderstorm. I was felled in Paris, blown to France by gentle winds of desire, by love for my wife, by dissatisfaction with the choices I hadn't made. I was uprooted in Paris, befuddled by the disorientation of facing a life governed only by my choices.

I think, now, France awakened the first glimmers of political action. I might describe it as the nuance of conversations with the French, who declared their love and admiration of Americans but their hatred for our government. These were the days of "Freedom Fries," lies about WMDs, and the French as the most useful political punching bag for American right-wing ascendency. I might describe that awakening as the recognition that politics, for the French, is part of the air. Spirited discussion isn't an insult or violation of decorum. In that openness, I could see the problem of American manners, where we refuse to talk about things so they fester into great rifts.

George W. Bush wasn't Donald Trump. But the fierce activation of nationalism associated with post-9/11 politics established a politically convenient way to strengthen the barriers between American electoral factions. In this environment, American patriotism, perversely, refuses to allow a separation between person and government. In America, you have to choose a side. With us or against us.

* * *

I am thinking now about connections to the past, or origins, and landscape and the way we are rooted, in America, to deep layers of exile. Few Americans can claim generational nativity to the land of North America, and those who can are the most politically silenced. Those who scream the loudest about land and blood and self-righteousness have slender claim, roots that have barely poked the soil despite their fierce provocations of making the land they claim as theirs great again.

* * *

At the confluence of Poland and Slovakia, we'd been told the water was high, the river swollen by weeks of heavy summer rain. I expected white water, something far quicker than the slight current of this shallow flow. Instead, we sat in shallow wooden boats, each a series of flattened canoes lashed together.

At the helm, a weathered Pole wore traditional costume for the benefit of the tourists in the boat. Periodically, he pressed a long staff into the gravel bottom and pressed the boat forward. Satisfied with our course, he squatted on the edge of the boat and plucked his burning cigarette from between the slats. He drew slowly, then offered clouds of smoke that drifted along the boat into our faces. Each cigarette diminished slowly, down to his fingertips until he flicked the butt between the boards of the raft, where it drowned in the Dunajec and floated beneath us. We drifted in that manner for two hours, slowly winding our way from one country to the other, repeatedly crossing the border between Slovakia and Poland, floating the division of my family origins. My father took photos and remarked on the beauty of Slovakian churches. My mother sat quietly, drawing in the sheer faces of Polish rock carved by the steady rub of the river.

The day before, my father and I had walked that same border, higher up, toeing the rocks of a ten-foot path cut across the ridge at Kasprowy Wierch. Creeping fog reduced a clear July afternoon into ethereal clouds, driving many mountaintop visitors to the ski lodge café and simply erasing the view of the rest. I watched my father lean into his walking stick. Polish ski slopes lay to our left, a thousand feet of Slovakian mountain valley to our right. He joked that he might just head that way, set off down the slope into the homeland and seek out lost cousins in Bratislava. Moments later, he spied a pink-purple wild flower just off the ridge top, maybe ten feet down into Slovakia. He pinned his walking stick between loose stones, hung on, and bent over with his camera. While he teetered over the flower, I took my own photo, of him. If he lost his balance and slid into the chasm, at least I'd have a shot of his last moments.

A few days later, my mother hired a driver to take the two of us on a trip to the graveyards of her great-grandparents, Polish peasants who sent their young children across the ocean to Chicago in search of a future beyond struggle. Eventually we found the Polish village, a scattered collection of ramshackle houses more or less nearby the church. "Village" suggests too much. The word evokes the alpine architecture of Zakopane, the tiny ski resort just a few hours south where my father and I had hiked the border. "Village" implies a romantic tableau of thatch, ruddiness, and nostalgic simplicity. From a distance, the draft horses we watched pull a wagonload of cut hay supported such a notion. Up close, the rusty satellite dishes planted in muddy front yards demonstrated that horses are, in fact, simply cheaper than cars.

Our driver leaned against the fender of his car while my mother and I climbed into the hillside cemetery overlooking the church there in Niedzwiedz. She unfolded a piece of notepaper, checking the precise handwriting for names we hoped to find on gravestones. Her great-grandmother had been buried here long ago, before the Germans and before the Communists and before the old church had burned to the ground. We walked among the graves, earthen mounds here in Poland, six feet long, a couple feet wide, the bones lying not far beneath us. In some places, richer dead folk lay in concrete vaults surrounded by shining votives and silken flowers. In the older part of the graveyard, where we walked back and forth among the markers, we squinted to make out names on metal crosses, realizing that caustic rain had long since erased legibility.

Here, the paths were choked by weeds, and I sometimes tripped on the raised earth of unseen graves. It was soon clear that we'd not find what we'd come for. No one had been left to tend this grave, and so the weeds had done the job in their own way. My mother's grandmother had been sent away from her own mother in 1899, shipped off to Chicago when she was only fourteen in a Poland occupied, then, by empires from Prussia and Austria and Russia. The farmland had been destroyed, and the Poles were starving. This had been the best choice. Scrape together enough money to secure slow passage across the ocean, send a child away, where at least there might be a chance, where graves might at least be tended and not forgotten.

I had intended to leave a token in the graveyard, to lay a pencil on the grave of my great-great-grandmother as recognition of the parts of her that I carried within myself. Instead, I crouched among the whorled roots of an old oak in the center of the graveyard, then pressed the pencil deep into the earth, where it would melt, eventually, into soil.

* * *

How do you work to love what actually sucks? I don't know how to put this better. It's not something you can say as a political candidate because admitting truths of struggle is to out yourself as a traitor of place.

The greatest travesty of politics is that it can teach us to hate ourselves, as in hating our whole self as individuals and members of a collective. At least, this is the politics of where I am from, as I see it. We don't matter, even to ourselves, because we can only see the nostalgic toxicity of what we never were. We are defined and come to define ourselves within the bankrupt social imagery used to sell us out.

Coal keeps the lights on, for example. That slogan, which appears on billboards from time to time, near wounded landscapes and decaying small towns ravaged by an industry that never worried much about the lights of those who toiled within it. Look, one of the wealthiest people from my hometown made a fortune in junkyards, buying up abandoned equipment and railroads and even whole towns. How can we understand ourselves in any way other than living in metaphor?

So I push it, and I say: Let's consider succession, the ecological sort, in the context of politics, as a way to imagine what once was and might be again. This requires, of course, a fair assessment of what was, which demands a reckoning of the long history of disturbance in our region, even our nation. We have been felled since the beginning. The so-called conservative love of the imagined past is in fact just another storm of destruction.

We're not done being destroyed, perhaps. I don't know that I can call this hope, but I might be able to imagine it as a glimmer of something. An opportunity to admit truths, and look toward different imagery as a source of our collective faith. Because, despite the avowed hatred of poetry in American political life, everything we do responds to poetry, is poetry. We live our lives in response to the stories we tell, and worse to the ones told about us. It's certainly hard, though, when you're living in the middle of the narrative. There's no resolution, and it's unclear where the story is headed.

I love where I am from, at least sometimes. I mean this as a reconciliation of place, really, as an exploration of what has been harmed and how and, instead of abandoning home, finding a way for it to be itself again, maybe for the first time.

My point in running for office boils down to a crystalline slogan that, probably, I should have used as an official campaign point: Please give a shit about us.

As well, please read some Walt Whitman and some Ross Gay and some Crystal Wilkerson and some Janisse Ray. Please understand that we all get churned in the same blender in rural America. No one gives a shit about us, neither the GOP nor the DNC. They've got us right where they want us. Powerless. Broke. Begging for the scraps of an American dream long ago tattered by coalitions of big business politicians. If no one runs, those who support the harm get to win quietly. It still hurts that others see slag heaps as a sign of economy instead of a warning against further damage.

* * *

A few years ago, Wendell Berry traveled from his Kentucky farm for a rare public appearance at the college where I teach. As part of the kickoff for a sustainable forestry conference, Berry anchored a panel of experts on timber management. My father drove two hours from his own reclaimed farm, and the two of us snuck into an auditorium filled with an odd collection of timber men and women: potbellied farmers, scruffy axe men, some hipster loggers wearing flannel, dirty work boots, and retro eyeglasses. My father urged me to the front row, where I felt old feelings of embarrassment flush. This was my turf, new turf, as I'd only joined this particular faculty nine months before, and in some ways I resented the ease at which I returned to the simple role of son, settling into the front row where he wanted to sit.

I counted Berry's appearance here as both miracle and gift. I had only recently started reading his work with a mature eye while preparing to teach my environmental literature class. I'd been struck reading him, both by the utter majesty of his writing and by uncanny coincidence. The farm I grew up on had been my father's reclamation project, a choked hundred acres left behind when a developer lost his fortune in Vegas, not unlike the salvage job Berry had engaged in the south. I'm not sure why it came as such a surprise, then, when my father informed me that

Berry was one of his and, particularly, one of my mother's favorite authors. That Berry so rarely travels for events like that conference barely factored into this calculus of shock.

But he had a friend in the area, another member of the panel in fact, who runs a forest conservancy founded on principles of sustainable timber management. So many people move away from our Pennsylvania woods that many others inherit forests for which they have little use. Often, clear-cuts present a precise and rapid execution of the estate. The conservancy offers a different option: horse-driven timbering that includes careful, laborious selection of trees. As the panel made clear, they do not high-grade: This describes a responsible-sounding practice that, in reality, mows down all of the healthiest, most biologically robust trees, and leaves the spindly weak stuff behind. The rhetoric of high-grading describes this as a way to give little trees a chance to grow stronger while, instead, such practice removes strong genetics from the gene pool and leaves only the weakest behind. As a forestry professor from Penn State described on the stage, such cutting is analogous to a dairy farmer slaughtering all of his good milkers to give the poor producers a chance to make more milk.

By adopting horses as timber vehicles, the conservancy also sought to protect the land from ruts, erosion, and the kind of ruptured soil that machines cannot avoid, thereby preserving the perpetual harvest of timber in much the same way Berry writes of redeeming sloped fields with horse-drawn plows in "The Making of a Marginal Farm." But suffice it to say, neither this timber conservancy nor Wendell Berry were proposing a human-free succession. Quite obviously, their forests are not being allowed to succumb to inertia. They are managed, held back from climax states by one of the chief ecological disturbances that ends so-called primary succession—the *original* process of development in a forest—and creates conditions favorable for secondary succession.

Viewed through the lens of the panel on that stage, and through that of my father as well, the presence of humans in the process of succession is less disturbance than partnership. Theirs are philosophies that seek to avoid the binary of environment versus human, that trumpet the merits of responsible use and human membership within the environment itself. And, really, that strikes me as a prudent stance. As Lynn White, Jr. and many other ecological scholars have noted, the separation of human and nature is, in a sense, a pathology rooted within deeply embedded Judeo-Christian concepts of natural dominion.

Perhaps the ideal forest is not one of climax, then, not one of rigid homogeneity but, instead, a forest that makes room for human beings within the ecological exchange. We manage and are managed by forests. We are part of the forests, acting upon the environment to alter the balance, for sure, but allowing ourselves to also be acted upon by the environment to give us balance. Sustainability and ethics occur when we recognize both our position as part of ecology and that forest preservation, like all environmentalism, is really, at heart, self-preservation.

*　*　*

Parts of the Robert Frost Interpretive Trail, located in the Green Mountain National Forest near Ripton, Vermont, run alongside the South Branch of the Middlebury River, which drains water from Bread Loaf Mountain into the farm valley below. Several years ago, I walked that trail with a small group led by John Elder, a retired professor from nearby Middlebury College. Poles flank the trail at irregular intervals, upon which are fastened Robert Frost poems, some famous and some less so. Visitors walk the landscape described in the poems, and in some small way have a chance to gain different perspective into a body of literature that, too often, loses power through its familiarity.

On that walk, John described the process of the land we observed: how a pond that had, not too many years ago, been open and was now filling in with bog plants, had been so changed by the washout of a beaver pond; how Forestry Service crews periodically mow and torch the shrubs that take root in the meadows beside the trail; and how the wide barrens below spruce trees are secured by the tannic acids released by the trees themselves, who secure their fortune by poisoning away other botanical competitors.

The idea of the trail, John explained, was to allow visitors to see the Vermont that Frost would have seen, to in some small way fix in time the stages of Frost's landscape. Nature rarely allows such grooming without a fight, of course, a fact clear enough from the river. Just a year before this walk, Hurricane Irene pounded up the East Coast, flooding into Vermont with a rare inland fury. The force of water rushing down so many mountain streams ripped banks away, knocked trees asunder, even recarved the channel in many places in many waterways. The evidence of that disturbance is clear enough on the South Branch, where what not long ago would have been just a gentle stream is now a gentle stream flanked by wide expanses of large gravel and sheer mud cliffs. Uprooted trees litter the banks in places, and it's not hard to be amazed at the sheer volume of water that must have coursed through this place.

A day before the walk, I sat on the grassy lawn in front of Frost's nearby writing cabin while John addressed a group of writers gathered for the Bread Loaf Writers Conference. While the intense August sun quickly dowsed rivulets from my neck and back, John gracefully stood under a sugar maple and described the forest history of Vermont. With the exception of the Upper Peninsula of Michigan, he explained, no part of the United States was timbered more thoroughly than Vermont. While the state seems to exist in a gloried, untouched, pristine state of forest, it, in fact, has been clear-cut—to bare earth—twice. First went the hardwood, felled for potash and charcoal, cleared away for farms. When the farms failed, in grew the conifers, which were ripped free and, just like in my own Pennsylvania, then the contemporary mixed forest finally grew in.

In a section of *Reading the Mountains of Home* fittingly called "Succession," Elder writes of the one-hundred-year-long cycles through which old farm fields grow back into forests. This cycle "offers redemptive visions of inclusiveness," he suggests. "There is a grand logic of transformation, meaningful to the thoughtful observer, but always transcending the limited human purposes with which we might identify one phase or another of the whole." In a way, he speaks softly against the notion of the human control of the environment. Such an enterprise is hardly more than hubris, revealed in the folly of clearing Vermont mountains to plant farms in a glaciated landscape devoid of topsoil. There can be no human control in such a situation since the action of farming fails to recognize the capacity of the land. Control, here, is illusory, a fantasy of domination wrecked by the relentless desire of forests to be forests.

I think of these words when I think about the eroded banks of the South Branch, where the glacial till has been laid bare by the powerful forces of tropical weather. I've always been drawn to water, moving and still, fresh or salt. And even in its torrents, I've never quite been able to muster anger. Instead, I recall wonder and excitement when the stream in our lower pasture used to bubble muddy gushes after summer thunderstorms. At normal levels, that small stream offered a perfect site for childhood wading and crayfish catching, but in the storms its capacity breached the banks, spread across the flat edges of the pasture, bypassed the corrugated steel culverts the gas drilling company had installed to keep their access road intact.

That's a redemption to me, that alone. Maybe three times a summer, the tiny stream refused to submit to the gas company's will, something my father could never avoid doing, thanks to subsurface rights controlled by a long-gone, out-of-state former owner. Water finds its own course, as it did in our Pennsylvania pasture, and as it so clearly did in the South Branch of the Middlebury River. Water is perpetual, and so too its frictions. The storms of Irene knocked out power for weeks, collapsed roads for months, wreaked havoc on the state in ways that were difficult and painful for residents to deal with.

But looking down the South Branch, feet on the wooden bridge over the water, listening to John recall a story of guiding the Dalai Llama on that very trail, the fallen trees on the bank evoke something other than despair. "A fallen log is something for hope," he writes in "Succession," "A hope, rather, for involvement in the grand pattern that connects."

* * *

When my father visited us in Paris, he and I visited the Musée de le Chasse et de la Nature, and I've long wondered why a moment from that trip lingers within me, frequently calling out as if to say, *This is important.* We went because my father loves hunting and nature, the specific charge of that museum. But at the end of our tour, we turned into a small room filled with oil paintings of laundry blowing in the breeze. This was a random installation, some exhibit outside the usual scope of the Musée. Several of the city's museums had rooms like this that summer, space set aside for contemporary artists to show their work.

I remember the bulk of the museum as dusty, quiet in a moldering sort of way. Bald spots shone through many of the taxidermy mounts on display. I remember the paintings of laundry as fluttering in my heart, some breeze at that moment separating what I valued in the museum, perhaps, from what my father valued, even though everything of value lay under the same verse. The exhibit staked its own claim in a new habitat of artistic self-definition. The artwork fit, not because it was of the same subject as the rest of the Musée, but because its presence expanded the scope of the place.

Jozef Paczoski, a Polish ecologist writing in Slavic, died the year my father was born, in 1941. Among his achievements was an early understanding of the way plants affect their own surroundings, that they are not merely subject to the land they are born into. Instead, through various mechanisms, they shape their environment, make it for themselves.

As a child of both Polish and Slavic heritage, I'm drawn to think of these ideas as somehow embedded within me though I'd like to think also they are embedded within all of us. This is the potential that lay within my moment among laundry paintings in an obscure Parisian museum. In some way, the moment of vision, when these fluttering sheets appeared around a corner, was prepared for by the departing Polish and Slovakian children of my ancestry. This, I think, at least partly explains the resonance of that moment. As Paczoski understood, an organism can affect its own place within a community. An individual can alter the trajectory of succession, even long after the process has begun. Hidden winds fluttered those paintings, and the breeze wrapped around some spot inside of me, too.

* * *

You run for office in the middle of a life. You run because you have tried your whole life to fit into rural Pennsylvania, your home. It's never worked, not fully. You are trapped always in a middle space, never quite, and not really, too much this and not enough that. Politics are not life, and they are not you. This versus that, and an annual consumption of the lives we all spend at the hands of mathematical constructs of victory. 60–40, 60–40, 60–40.

The summer of 2020 feels like it should have been an inflection point. It should have changed things. Covid was a meteor dropping into a quiet village. *Deus ex machina*, the mighty hand of celestial intervention reaching out to make it so we can't continue on the path we'd been trudging. Yet, of course, you know what happened. You have been living through the Age of Covid, too. You have witnessed the politics of the pandemic, the perverse invocations of a twisted version of Thoreau, wicked self-reliance encouraging the perpetuity of inequality, economy, economy, economy. Unvaccinated zealots crowding local hospitals. Bullies trying to legislatively rip masks off the faces of vulnerable school-children. The relentless drumbeats of denial. The political usefulness of all of this. 2020 should have broken open the narrative and helped us all see the world as it has been laid out before us. Suffering. Abandonment. Flatlined hope.

2020 was a violent election, long before the insurrection at the Capitol. Trump flags waving in yards. The violence of rural orthodoxy. The dark antipoetic vision of rural "freedom" predicated on the destruction of imagined enemies. The violence of exclusion as an expressed desire to exile, to cast out those who refuse to submit. Love it or leave it, words always dripping with venom. And that has worked out awfully well for those in control of the economy because the vast spaces of American rurality are seen only as a company town. If you live here, you owe your body to the machine.

That's the whole deal. You are here. I am here. Knowing that
is something even though the machinery of politics tries its
damnedest to build shibboleths of isolation. You can't be from
here, not really, if you aren't willing to close your eyes and hurtle
your life into the maw. The greatest frustration of politics is
knowing that, and knowing it is simple, and everyone knows it.
Yet knowing has never been enough to change anything at all
because the interests of politics reduce to the distortions of partisan bases. The summer of 2020 should have made it all so clear,
so very clear. The election of 2020 should have been an obvious
of demarcation. But it wasn't. So we're all left here, together,
struggling and trapped and unable to imagine our way out of it
without running afoul of the very machinery that wants to prevent our escape.

I have been feeling a great fleeing lately. That's middle age, I
think, an urge to go back in time to fix what seems broken or
even just try out paths abandoned. But my desire seems like a
deeper sort of lament. Maybe it's the residue of alienation and
broken connections, a general sense of brokenness. Things went
haywire somewhere, in the ways things always go haywire,
between the time I was sure of things and the time I wasn't.

Yes, this sounds like middle age. It also sounds like politics, or
at least sounds like political desire. At some level, every politician
runs to repair something they perceive as decayed. I think every
politician runs on their wounds too. I mean this both narratively
and psychologically, the way we flawed human beings make so
many decisions in pursuit of the satisfaction of deeply felt voids,

insults, injuries. I go back to the idea of bullies, even if so many bullies in politics actually operate more like the bullied trying to mitigate their torment. I have learned enough about the incumbent I tried to beat to understand his own harm, how he legislates like a bullied high school outcast in a constantly frustrated attempt to earn favor from the people who rejected him when he was a boy. Your state rep is probably the same, and your senator, and your governor, and your mayor. I mean, aren't we all?

All of this is to say that running for office isn't necessarily a healthy impulse in the context of midlife. Running for office because you want to fix things, sure, makes sense. But a good therapist is going to tell you that you can't fix yourself, or rather you can't fix your relationship to the place around you, by becoming a state representative. We'd do well to read all politicians in the context of foundational wounds. We'd do well to think about what they're trying to fix about themselves, about who they were and how that hurt them and how they seek power to restore order to themselves and call it "public service."

While I freely admit I am a fanboy of the literary, I am deeply committed to the idea of narrative as a tool of reconstruction. As David Mura writes of my favorite genre, "Memoir is a reenvisioning of the past self and thus coming to terms with the limitations of one's past self."

Or, as I teach my own students, we write memoir always with multiple selves on the page, always at least two. At a minimum, there's the experiential self, who lived the action on the page, and there's the reflective self, who actively authors the interrogation of meaning. When we write, we negotiate that deep past, in fact relive it in our own minds, as a way to make sense of what that past meant both then and continues to mean, now.

The dynamic of reflective narrative is as powerful for a region as it is for an individual writer as it is for a politician as it is for a failed candidate. If we don't approach lived experience or history with the approach of the memoirist, we risk repeating narratives regardless of their impact. Worse, we risk making decisions about our present day in lockstep to the narratives—often false ones— we have internalized despite their distortions.

I am a rural boy. I am a rural man. I learned lessons as a boy that make it harder to negotiate being the kind of rural man I want to be. I learn lessons now that make it harder still, seeing how the apparent rigidity of the term *rural* dictates so much of what frustrates my days living in the region where I was born. As much as it hurts to be exiled—as much as it hurts, in my case, to lose an election—it's somehow worse and unavoidable to begin building one's own act of exile.

* * *

Midway through the walk around the Robert Frost Trail, John Elder stopped beside a marker bearing the words of the poet's famous "Stopping By Woods on a Snowy Evening." The day had been sublime so far, a clarified blue sky, low humidity, pleasantly warm. Around Bread Loaf, I had just the day before noticed the first tinges of scarlet on a few low branches, and already the crisp nights felt very much like autumn at home. The walk, too, had been nothing short of wonderful. John's gentle demeanor combined with his prodigious intellect to produce the quiet force of truth. He spoke of Frost in ways I was unaccustomed, redeeming him for me with a certain simplicity of purpose. Frost was a great observer of nature, John told us, and ecologically spot on. I suppose, for me, this rediscovery of Frost echoed what John writes in "Aji" about his own study of Vermont natural history: "Good things have come in roundabout and unanticipated ways." I should mention this, too: My father likes Robert Frost, perhaps the only poet he might choose to read for pleasure.

There we stood, at the halfway point, beside the marker, while John described a group of Vermonters reciting the famous poem aloud while traveling with groups from several other nations. He invited my own group to do so, and more than a few knew the poem well enough to oblige in the choral reading. And as surprised as I might have been by their memories—I wasn't able to muster the words to speak alongside them—I was more surprised to find my throat catching near the end of the poem, when the speaker's horse

> gives his harness bells a shake
> To ask if there is some mistake.
> The only other sound's the sweep
> Of easy wind and downy flake.

The group finished, and I looked ahead at the peak of the distant ridge. We stepped forward, then stopped again soon near a clearing populated by wild berries. John described how bears will settle in to such patches, hunker down and take mighty sweeps with the paws until every last berry has been consumed. And there, in that moment, suddenly, I felt myself as a child, walking behind a stream of college students, my father at the helm, explaining this biological function or that, pausing beside a stream, boot on a rock in that fashion I know so well. I could hear my father's voice, a projecting authority, not without tenderness, as he pinched a caddis fly nymph between his fingers and explained the life cycle, how the young changes over time into the adult, who in turn provides young for another generation.

I lagged behind the group on the Frost Trail, my composure slipping. I felt my eyes well up, flooded from what, in the moment, was an unidentifiable sense of significance. I thought of my father, and in the next moment of our first and then, only, son, of walking trails together. I thought of the salve of walking, the succor of Thoreau's wilderness, of how much my first son has loved to walk since he learned how. He tracked circles around and around and around our house, reaching his arms into my hands and declaring, "Daddy, walk." I think, now, of our second son also, a vibrant boy always in motion, often telling breathless stories accompanied by short peregrinations around the living room.

Daddy, walk. Daddy, walk. Daddy, let me tell you a story. Indeed, the succession of myself as the son who walked with his father, who will continue to walk with his father, who will be the father who walks with his sons, who somehow on that August afternoon walked with all of them, though two were

500 miles away and one a year from his own arrival onto this earth. Succession ignores the boundaries of time and space, when we learn to recognize the reality of hope, of how we are akin to the plants who shape our own environment, how we are doing it even when the invasive creeping vetches of our landscapes work so very hard to choke us out. Yes, always, this book is about politics, and the metaphors we can't quite see, and the ones that might save us if we can just recognize them, hold onto them, nurture them into being.

To be uprooted, then, or worse to be told you must be uprooted against your own will and nativity, is a dire act of political violence. It is being told you don't matter, you don't belong, you are out of step, you do not belong. Let me fold in another analogy, that of the mysterious mycelial communication network beneath the forest, how the mighty fungal warriors break down and refurbish the soil, and how they also appear to work to secretly pass messages between lonely trees.

Let us be the fungus. Let us be the lonely trees. Let us put faith in the invisible functions of geological time, and positive progress, and the ecological wisdom of Barack Obama's arrow of history bending always toward progress.

"A fallen log is something for hope," John Elder writes, and I wonder now about the infinite regression of fallen logs, fertile spaces that litter forests literal and imagined. The best promises we can keep are to make space for such logs, always, to walk among them when we can. And I know, too, that the making of such space is the true nature of inertia. It is the source of real stability, that of our world and our own lives. I do not wonder about the infinite regression of hope. I am convinced by John Elder, and Frost, and my father, and my sons, and by the stories of ancestors who sought to change their family lot by boat and by degree. I am convinced that we walk always in forests alongside those who came before us.

ELEVEN

IMAGINATION

The results of my own exercise, as a writer and a candidate and a rural American:

If I could meet my child self atop the family farm, on a quiet cold day, either beneath the usual gray ceiling or, better, when a rare clear blue winter day crisps everything, rime frost on the fields now turned to prairie grass, I'd want to find him beneath the peeled smooth surface of an old dead oak near the property line. There's the power plant on the horizon. Here's the gas well road, upon which my middle-aged ghost walks.

The skeletal tree would be discordant, for him, because if he remembered it at all, he'd remember it as a lush green, boyhood memories rooted in summer and the tree not yet a remnant, when he lived here. And, I don't know, would I want to approach and offer him a warning? Would I want to frame out the future he would face, one built not on trauma—he doesn't need to know about that, not right now—but on the quiet grasping fingers of rage I know he's already starting to feel?

Junior high. That's how old I am. I can tell by the lean body, angular like the oak, sharp shoulder blades. Ninth grade, probably, finding some sense of himself in music, as a kid actor in kid school plays, occasional flashes of interest in writing words and the usual boredom and frustration at the words he's forced to read in school. I know he's afraid because that's not so much a memory but a perpetual sense that I've never been able to shake. But fear, like trauma, is a word too common here. It's not trembling or panic, but the shadow sense that the world around us is animated by violence.

Violence fills the horizon, visible through the branches of the dead tree. The generating station, puffing the exhaust of burnt coal high in the air. A permanent fixture on the skyline, yes, but also an unshakeable anchor for the whole godforsaken region. I know he feels that. This is memory. A growing sense, even as a boy, that simple answers won't work, even my father's emphasis on conservation, and prudence, and efficiency. None of these is really enough. They will be, for him—the boy of me—the future of a region in decline, a tethering to a melancholy slow collapse that needs to just happen, but won't. Or, worse, a future marked by angry political resistance to new options. Because that dead tree, the one he must be reaching to brush, seems like a relic and a casualty and a symbol and just a tree. Frozen in death, beautiful when backlit by the sun, but still a marker of what once was in a landscape marred by what has been done to it, and us, repeatedly.

That's my deep anger. That when we hear a new choice, too few are willing to listen. Too many prefer the consequence of death to the possibility of rebirth. There's no poetic way to write the future when the past holds us so tightly, won't let us go. This is Appalachia. This is the Rust Belt. It is the consequence of living here, that our very existence cannot separate from the violence done to us.

Well, it could. That's the real source of my anger. It so easily could. But we are steeped in coal, in gas, in industrial service to those who profit on our own demise, sold out by politicians who can't see us. We've become more or less the decaying organic matter that makes the energy for the rest of the country. Might as well be. And I want to see that as the metaphor of anger, that the people of my region know that, feel that, resent that, and lash out because they want better for him, that kid in front of me, the me who will become a worn out middle-aged man with a bad eye, who feels stuck every damn day in this place that he also loves too much to abandon. Who decides it's worth risking becoming a politician. Who loses.

I want to sit down beside that tree. I want to sit in front of my boyhood. Each of us could lean against the trunk of the oak, find the angle of hope. Not south toward the power plant. Or north toward the bypass. Or west toward the closest brine tank. Maybe east, toward the sunrise, and also toward the corner of the farm where, if you look low enough, you can avoid seeing the strip mine scar of the distant hill. I want to gaze there, with myself, and explain to him the bubbling rage he will feel. I want to tell him about the futures that could be, here in Appalachia, in America, in a world broken by the expectation of violence.

I want to tell him how beautiful the Capitol can be.

I want to tell him how you can feel joy in the attempt.

I want to tell him it's okay to leave.

I want to tell him it's okay to stay.

I want to tell him about the day he will drive home from Harrisburg after becoming a candidate, about the late afternoon somewhere between the Susquehanna River and the small town of Port Royal, about the gray low clouds breaking open, and the shafts of sunlight. You will call your father, and you will chat about the election, and your father's baritone pride will sound like hope itself.

How we lose can become different, a field ready to burst with summer flowers, flitting grasshoppers, the rustling of quiet futures ready to emerge.

I want to tell myself we will face losing, but that's the hope we cannot allow to become an ending.

A POETICALLY POLITICAL READING LIST

Abbey, Edward. *Desert Solitaire: A Season in the Wilderness.*
New York: Ballantine Books, 1971.

Baudrillard, Jean. *Simulacres et Simulation.* Paris: Éditions
Galliêe, 1981.

Berry, Wendell. *Essays 1969–1990.* Edited by Jack Shoemaker.
New York: Library of America, 2019.

Bugan, Carmen. *Poetry and the Language of Oppression: Essays
on Politics and Poetics.* Oxford: Oxford University
Press, 2021.

Carson, Rachel. *Silent Spring.* Boston: Houghton Mifflin,
1962.

Elder, John. *Reading the Mountains of Home.* Cambridge, MA:
Harvard University Press, 1999.

Foucault, Michel. *Discipline & Punish: The Birth of the Prison.*
Translated by Alan Sheridan. New York: Random
House, 1995.

Frost, Robert. *The Poetry of Robert Frost: The Collected Poems,
Complete and Unabridged.* Edited by Edward Connery
Lathem. New York: Henry Holt, 1979.

Gay, Ross. *The Book of Delights*. Chapel Hill, NC: Algonquin Books of Chapel Hill, 2019.

Hirschfield, Jane. *Nine Gates: Entering the Mind of Poetry*. New York: HarperCollins, 1997.

Kleeb, Jane. *Harvest the Vote: How Democrats Can Win Again in Rural America*. New York: Ecco, 2020.

Kundera, Milan. *The Art of the Novel*. New York: Harper-Collins, 1988.

Leopold, Aldo. *A Sand County Almanac*. Oxford: Oxford University Press, 1949.

Lerner, Ben. *The Hatred of Poetry*. New York: Farrar, Straus and Giroux, 2016.

Litman, Amanda. *Don't Just March, Run for Something: A Real-Talk Guide to Fixing the System Yourself.* New York: Atria Books, 2017.

Liu, Eric. *Become America: Civic Sermons on Love, Responsibility, and Democracy*. Seattle: Sasquatch Books, 2019.

Mura, David. *A Stranger's Journey: Race, Identity, and Narrative Craft in Writing*. Athens: University of Georgia Press, 2018.

Oliver, J. Eric, Shang E. Ha, and Zachary Callen. *Local Elections and the Politics of Small-Scale Democracy*. Princeton, NJ: Princeton University Press, 2012.

Oliver, Mary. *A Poetry Handbook*. San Diego, CA: Harcourt, Inc., 1994.

Ray, Janisse. *Ecology of a Cracker Childhood*. Minneapolis, MN: Milkweed Editions, 1999.

Rove, Karl. *The Triumph of William McKinley: Why the Election of 1896 Still Matters*. New York: Simon & Schuster, 2015.

Ruefle, Mary. *Madness, Rack, and Honey: Collected Lectures*. Seattle: Wave Books, 2012.

Rukeyser, Muriel. *The Book of the Dead*. Reprint. Morgantown: West Virginia University Press, 2018.

Rukeyser, Muriel. *The Life of Poetry*. New York: Current Books, 1949.

Scafidi, Steve. *The Cabinetmaker's Window: Poems*. Baton Rouge: Louisiana State University Press, 2014.

Steingraber, Sandra. *Living Downstream: An Ecologist's Personal Investigation of Cancer and the Environment*. Cambridge, MA: De Capo Press, 2010.

Wallace, David Foster. *A Supposedly Fun Thing I'll Never Do Again: Essays and Arguments*. Boston: Little, Brown and Co., 1997.

Weaver, Michael Aafa. *Spirit Boxing*. Pittsburgh, PA: University of Pittsburgh Press, 2017.

White, Lynn. "The Historical Roots of Our Ecological Crisis." *Science* 155 (1967): 1203–1207.

Whitman, Walt. *Leaves of Grass*. 1855.

Wilkerson, Crystal. *Birds of Opulence*. Lexington: University Press of Kentucky, 2016.

Wright, James. *Collected Poems*. Middletown, CT: Wesleyan University Press, 1974.

Young, Dean. *The Art of Recklessness: Poetry as Assertive Force and Contradiction.* Minneapolis, MN: Graywolf Press, 2010.

Zagajewski, Adam. *Without End: New and Selected Poems.* Translated by Clare Cavanagh and Renata Gorczynski, Benjamin Ivry, and C. K. Williams. New York: Farrar, Straus and Giroux, 2002.